The Power is in the Connection

Taking your Personal and Professional Relationships to the NextLevel

Jane George-Surges

Ron Sukenick

ATTENTION: Schools and Corporations

"The Power is in the Connection" is available at quantity discounts with bulk purchase for educational, business, or sales promotional use.

Thinking of a live interpretation of this book?

Ron Sukenick and Jane George Surges are widely recognized speakers and trainers who give programs for corporations, organizations, and associations. Their presentations are known for practical information, humor and results. For further information about these informative and entertaining programs, please write to the addresses below.

Library of Congress Cataloging-in-Publication Data

Surges, Jane George
Sukenick, Ron
The Power is in the Connection
Includes Glossary and Index.
Trade paperback edition ISBN 0-9725960-4-6

Printed in the United States of America.

Cover Design by **Layout by** **Publishing and Printing by**

Printing PARTNERS

Ron Sukenick
Relationship Strategies Institute
www.relationshipstrategiesinstitute.com
rs@relationshipstrategiesinstitute.com
5443 North Arlington Ave.
Indianapolis, Indiana 46226 USA
317-216-8210

Jane George Surges
Training and Development Resources, Inc.
www.trainingdevelopmentresources.com
jgsurges@aol.com
www.netbeing.us
4255 Clarendon Rd.
Indianapolis, IN 46208
317-920-0188

10 9 8 7 6 5 4 3 2 1

Comment Section

"Wow. I am so impressed with what Ron Sukenick and Jane George-Surges are doing to really make a difference in personal and professional relationships. If you think you have seen, read, and done it all....think again. Success truly comes in all areas of our life if we are continuing to build relationships. Every day I am amazed at the blessings of networking. Many people just don't get it. With this book, you will! If you think you've read enough self-help books...think again."

Sally Brown
President/Ambassadair Travel Club and Ambassadors for Children

---

"Ron and Jane's insight into the relationship process is a fresh and welcomed approach."

"They have clearly described a place that you can come from in the world of networking. A book all Business Professionals need to read and embrace."

Hazel Walker
President, Crystal Synergies
Executive Director BNI Central IN

"People do business with people they know and trust and with people referred to them by people they know and trust. The Power is in the Connection *provides a process to help you easily get to know and be known by others and to begin and develop vital relationships."*

Lillian D. Bjorseth
Author, *Breakthrough Networking: Building Relationships That Last, 52 Ways to Break the Ice & Target Your Market*

"A practical and useful approach to taking networking to a completely new level! Ron Sukenick and Jane Surges have captured strategies for business and life that emphasize the importance of building relationships and connecting!"

Linda Rendleman
Founder, Business Women Connect

"I'm impressed!! Your book provides a thorough step-by-step approach for building, deepening and enjoying relationships. The world is changing so very fast and our current relationship models and ways of dealing with relationships are outdated."

"I believe your book will awaken something that we all long for in our professional and personal lives....the ability to establish connections that add depth and vitality!"

Gigi Sage
Creator - "The Power Connection" Workshop

"One's ability to connect and lay a solid person-to-person foundation for building relationships is paramount for success. We must teach the next generation of business professionals about building their business through networking and relationship building! Otherwise, we are graduating scores of young people with college degrees in business and marketing and not giving them one iota of training in an area that almost all business practitioners agree is most critical to the success of any enterprise."

Dr. Ivan Misner
Founder, BNI
Co-Author, *Masters of Networking*

"When I look back on my career, it is clear to me that I would have accomplished nothing without the relationships that I developed along the way."

Roger Dawson
Author, *Secrets of Power Negotiating*

"In my books on "Relationship Selling" I speak frequently about building relationships before you need them. This goes hand in hand with another concept I espouse, "Reputation Management." When we determine in advance what relationships and reputation we want to have, then we can shift our focus to do those things that lead to such outcomes."

"The true potential in relationships comes from trust, respect and a desire to do good things for each other."

Jim Cathcart
Author, *The Eight Competencies of Relationship Selling*

"Working with Ron on several occasions has been an absolute pleasure. He lives and breathes the strategies included in The Power is in the Connection. *I'm recommending the book to everyone in my network!"*

Darrell Ross
Contributing Author, *Masters of Networking*

"I see business relationships becoming more and more what I call "purposeful" in that both parties look out for the success of the other. Relationships are within a systemic mesh that requires all aspects to be excellent for any aspect to be excellent."

Tom Lane
Author, *The Way of Quality*

"The desire to connect and contribute is basic to who we are as human beings. Networking is not a technique; it is a way of relating that can change a relationship, create an opportunity and enhance the world. Ron and Jane's research and strategies clearly support the value of making strong connections."

Donna Fisher
Author, *Power Networking, People Power, Professional Networking for Dummies* and *Five Keys to Building Relationships Online*

"As someone who's been in chamber of commerce work for nearly thirty years, I can tell you EVERYTHING is about relationships! The more tools a person has to enhance relationships with other individuals and organizations, the better chance that person has to be successful. Ron Sukenick really walks the talk on networking. This book will benefit anyone in the relationship business!"

John S. Myrland
President, Greater Indianapolis Chamber of Commerce

"Ron and Jane really understand that the way to experience all kinds of relationships is to BE in the flow of them, not to analyze them, but to truly experience them moment to moment."

Dr. Deri Ronis, Ph.d
Author - *Soulful Love*

"Jane and Ron, I am inspired by your focus to create "mutually supportive, purposeful, creative, and rewarding" relationships. You truly bring who you are to what you do."

"The philosophy of NetBeing is clearly a creation of passion and purpose; it is also a road map for where we must go as human beings in this next, most challenging century. I love your focus on interdependence and relationshifts as central to understanding and honoring our basic, underlying connectedness and to maximize that energy to develop synergy. It has always been my belief that emotions are really Energy in MOTION and to consciously align purpose with action creates personal and shared reality."

Karl D. LaRowe MA, LCSW
International Speaker and Trainer
Mental Health Investigator and Examiner
Mental Health Delegate to China

"Jane Surges and Ron Sukenick understand the power of belongingness and human connection in deep and authentic ways. Even better, they are masterful teachers for helping others realize their potential for building these essential relationships."

Kathleen Brehony, Ph.D.
Autor of *Living a Connected Life:*
Creating and Maintaining Relationships That Last

Contents

Foreword

When my friend, Ron Sukenick, asked me to write the Foreword to this book, *The Power is in the Connection,* I cringed. So many books, so many ideas, so many prescriptions for success; the thought of dealing with yet another one was overwhelming to me.

Fortunately, I relented. And I'm glad I did. This book is a breath of fresh air. Finally, someone has addressed the subject of networking in an original and authentic way.

In a way that gets to the bottom of the word, relationship, and brings that word to the top of the mind, to the top of the heart, to the top of the commitment one needs to make if a truly authentic relationship is going to be served between the person who is looking for something and the person who is being engaged.

Because isn't that how all relationships start out? Someone wants something? A fellow wants a wife; a woman wants a husband? A girl wants a boy; a boy a girl? A business wants a customer; a customer wants to find exactly the right business to serve his or her needs?

And isn't it true that most of us are pretty dismal when it comes to the process of communicating to someone else what we want? In fact, isn't it also true that just knowing what we want, and feeling justified in wanting it, is a skill few of us have developed? And not knowing what we want, how often do we pursue a relationship with one thought in mind, only to find when it's too late that even if we got what we thought we wanted, it was far from the truth of what we wanted? And what do we do then?

That's what this book is all about. It defines the essence of relationship, and the 15 strategies one can use (along with the 15 skills one needs to develop) in order to develop healthy, authentic, deeply productive relationships. Whether for the purpose of growing your business, or for the purpose of developing your career, or for the purpose of creating more profitable work, working with more exciting people, doing things you love to do, rather than things you don't, relationship is the vehicle.

Tall order for a personal improvement book. But this book does exactly that. And in a way that is thoroughly enjoyable to read, and thoroughly inspiring to use as a bridge between where you are presently, and where you want to be.

I'm sure you'll find this book to be as inspiring as I did. I'm sure you'll find more than you're looking for in it.

Thanks Ron and Jane, for asking me. And, thanks for your patience in waiting for my response. But, after all, isn't that what a good relationship is about?

Michael Gerber, Author
The E-Myth Books

Preface

Quality relationships, based on overlapping purpose and mutual support, form in multiple ways. Once formed, quality relationships open the mind and heart to vast possibilities.

In this book, *The Power Is In The Connection,* fifteen relationship strategies reveal the key ingredients to building strong relationships. Strategy by strategy the powerful but invisible ways in which connections, alliances and partnerships are built and supported are presented.

This book will leave you with renewed optimism and a realistic approach for relationship success.

Commit right now to building relationships as the forefront of all interactions.

Best of luck on your journey toward relationship success.

Let the journey begin.

Ron Sukenick Jane George-Surges

Acknowledgment

For helping me learn about the power of relationship, thank you for coming along and being teachers in my life...Gale Nigg and Chuck Surges...my children Jaq, Corey, Christine, Chuck III and their families...my parents, Jim and Marie George, and my thirteen sisters and brothers. Thank you to the many friends who've helped me along my journey, students, colleagues, clients, my writing group, and many others. Thank you to Theresa Nelson Chilson, my best friend from the first grade who spoke to me in Donald Duck language and made me laugh; my first important relationship outside of my family, Theresa taught me over the years the power and depth of an enduring friendship as it transforms and shifts time and time again.

Thank you to Phil Black, who in his uniqueness and erudite ways read every word of this book, encouraged me along the way, and contributed helpful insights and observations. And to Tom Lane, a heartfelt thanks for his caring, his ruthlessness, his infinite patience and his "silent self" to my life. Thanks also to Pam Weinantz who said of relationship, "…What we see as different processes, that if blended, not separated are fertile ground for an exciting next stage of growth."

I want to also say a special thanks to women. A relationship focus is not new to women. Women have nurtured relationships as the lifeblood central to everything including personal and professional success. World peace through relationship….ahhhh, yes, it is possible.

To my co-author, Ron, thank you for partnering with me on this creative ride!

And, for you the reader, thanks for your desire demonstrated in reading this book to create a world where relationship is one of ease…where caring for others is a mutual desire for each other's success and support, and is part of the everyday. I am blessed to work and learn with others in a continual process of going to greater depths. We learn about ourselves in relationship and with awareness we grow further along our personal path. Imagine a world where relationship is the touchstone for all that we do...

Jane George-Surges

Acknowledgment

Over the years, I have developed a passion for building and developing relationships with others. How this passion came about, and for all those people that helped along the way, accept my heartfelt thanks. I feel a deep sense of gratitude for the mentors that came along early in my life, for the teachers and guides who took the time to share their wisdom, and for the many personal and professional relationships throughout my life who taught me about the power of connection.

To my co-author, Jane George-Surges, you are the perfect writing partner for this book.

A lifetime of continued thanks to my family. To my Mother, Yetta Sukenick, who while no longer with us, still remains a major force and relationship in my life today. Both my children, Christine Elizabeth and Freedom Star for loving me along the way.

To my wife, Yvonne, who plays a major part in my continued inspiration in building the kinds of relationships I want for my life, I thank you. I know clearly that our relationship together will never end. And also to Yvonne, I will forever be grateful for your creativity, support, and insights.

I also want to thank all the readers of my first book, *Networking Your Way to Success* and workshop and seminar participants who helped me see and dig more deeply to get a glimpse of this next level that individuals want for their life--a flow between self and others based on a mutual relationship. And, for those of you reading this book now, thank you!

Ron David Sukenick

Acknowledgement from Jane and Ron

Special thanks to Emily Blumenfeld and Evan Walters who read the book along the way and provided thoughtful recommendations, and later edited the entire book helping us to remain consistent and to not lose our focus from start to finish.

Thank you to Jeff Robinson of Dezinehouse for his creative graphic design. Jeff captured the philosophy of the book through his design of the book cover and developed graphics that reflect the essence of each strategy in a thought provoking and thoughtful manner. This book truly reflects your work. Thank you to Mike Boler at First Quality Printing for printing of the first brochure describing this work allowing us a tangible handout as we began talking with others about this project. Thank you, Mike, for helping us make this project come to life. Thank you to Megan Van Petten and her team for web site development.

Thanks to Ron White at The Partnership Group and Choices Press. Especially to Melanie Lantz Albright, Laura Wilkes, Julie Anderson, and Donna Cambra who provided their creativity to the design, layout, editing, and publishing expertise as we moved forward with this work.

Thank you to Michael O'Brien and his team at Printing Partners, www.printingpartners.net, who helped bring this project to fulfillment.

We thank the many of you who submitted comments and continue to submit encouraging feedback. Your questions also helped us crystallize our thought processes.

Thank you to the many others early in this process and all the way to now. We couldn't have done it without you!

Jane and Ron

The Floor Plan

4th & top floor

The pinnacle, Strategy 15

3rd floor

Strategies eleven, twelve, thirteen & fourteen

2nd floor

Strategies eight, nine & ten

Main floor

Strategies four, five, six & seven

Foundation

Strategies one, two & three

How to Use the Book

Imagine for a moment easily making personal and professional connections with others. Imagine tapping into your skills naturally, and establishing contact with individuals along the way. The three parts of this book have been written to help you foster these very skills. Part One sets the foundation and underlying philosophy vital to developing and deepening quality relationships. Part Two lays out the strategies, and Part Three brings it all together.

Bring this book to life! As you read, make notes, complete the exercises, and develop an action plan to immediately put these strategies to use. This book provides tools that call for commitment, experimentation and continuous improvement. Every relationship is different and will require your ability to diagnose and determine which strategy to use.

THE FLOOR PLAN

Each strategy stands alone however ideally, you will best benefit when you begin with the first strategy--live life purposefully. From there, you can move about the book. Looking at the framework of this book as a four story building, you will find that the first three strategies are the foundation.

- The foundation of this process begins with you, your personal clarity, your inner life, your mindset, and your ability to internally embrace your interdependence with others. Strategies one, two, and three set the tone and direction for purposefully going forward into relationship.
- The main floor launches you into relationship with others with strategies four, five, six, and seven; focusing on your ability to listen with purpose, provide joyful experiences, attend to the smallest of detail, and create visibility.
- The second floor features strategies eight, nine, and ten and will stimulate your thinking about making the connection, responding to a Fast-paced world, and shortening learning curves.

- The third floor provides strategies eleven, twelve, thirteen, and fourteen to help you move into legendary status, choose technology, become a global partner, and look back at where you have been and relationships to reconnect with.

- The 4th and top floor is the pinnacle--encompassing continuous improvement in all aspects of your life. It is the ongoing enhancement, growth, and development of total self.

In the chapters that follow, personal experiences, both our own and those of others, reinforce the lessons of this book. Readers will gain from insights and experiences and expand the concept of relationship success to encompass all of life.

Until one is committed, there is hesitancy, the chance to draw back, always ineffectiveness concerning all acts of initiative and creation. There is one elementary truth…that the moment one definitely commits oneself, providence moves too. All sorts of things occur to help one that never would have otherwise occurred. A stream of events issues from the decision, raising in one's favor all manners of unforeseen incidents and meetings and material assistance which no person could have dreamed would have come his way. Whatever you can do or dream you can, begin it. Boldness has genius, power, and magic in it. Begin it now.

Johann Wolfgang Von Goethe

PART ONE
THE FOUNDATION

Attention to a Relationship Focus

Motivational experts in the last century proposed a timeless and sustaining theme in the study of motivation: human beings throughout the world, share fundamental needs. On a continuum from physiological and survival needs to reaching to realize full potential, the central element threading throughout is the need for affiliation. Human beings have a need to be in relationship.

What is relationship? Simply put, relationship is a flow of feeling. This flow of feeling may be between you and a higher source, between you and nature, between you and your environment, or between you and another person. In this flow, an opportunity exists to experience *connection.* With another there is an opportunity for individual and mutual growth and support. We, as human beings, affect and are affected by others, help and are helped. Individuals have the opportunity to reach individual potential far beyond what they are able to do on their own, and to co-create when truly engaged in relationship. As they say in Africa, it takes a village to raise a child. Attention to a relationship focus takes this premise to the next level--it takes a village to maximize individual potential! All of us need relationship to maximize our full potential!

How does this need for relationship play out in life? This book defines critical aspects that contribute to relationship satisfaction and success. A person is drawn into relationship based on the joy of interacting with another person who shares a similar view of the world and incorporates fun, ease, energy, reliability, and creativity into the interaction. When these characteristics exist in business relationships, overall satisfaction is enhanced *while* helping each other obtain financial and professional success and enjoyment.

Creating personal and dynamic success in all aspects of our lives, then, requires attention to building our relationship skills. The 21st Century is an unprecedented time. The pace of change is so rapid that working at multiple levels with a wide range of partners and with a multitude of associations is paramount. The biggest challenge most people face is the ability to successfully build the kinds of relationships necessary in order to have the kind of success to which they aspire.

You will learn established strategies that will help you create and strengthen your relationship building skills. These strategies are outlined in Part Two of this book. Here, for your consideration are underlying thinking and guiding principles:

- The 21st century calls for self-knowledge and directing one's own life. Hence our number one guiding principle is to take leadership in your life's direction. Consciously and constantly choose the direction of your life toward that which is most important to you.

- To effectively align your choices, your time, and your energy, you must live purposefully. To do this, you must know your life purpose.

- To be successful in building relationship with others, you must first start with building a successful relationship with yourself. Self-knowledge is the underpinning that helps you persist in the direction of relationship success.

- Multiple visions for your life exist. Futurists predict that in the 21st century, each of us will have many careers. Identifying and defining your life purpose is the foundation; clearly aligning your career visions to your life purpose will create the vitality that will help you sense and seize business partnerships and relationships in the now and in the future.

- A clear distinction between **Net***Being* and *Networking* exists. Networking provides a situational focus to gain competitive personal success and for individuals to connect with others to accomplish individual project tasks. In **Net***Being,* individual *purposes* overlap and a joint focus fosters mutual and multiple successes. **Net***Being* transforms networking contacts to a *relationship* focus through person-to-person connection. **Net***Being* links creativity, resources, and ideas, people-to-people in mutually supportive, rewarding, and *purposeful* relationships over a lifetime.

- Creating success for others along the way takes on a life of its own! Through helping others, tangible and intangible rewards create magical and mysterious outcomes for all parties.

- What you have traditionally done to satisfy customers is not enough. Individuals want a deeper connection! New ways of showing up today and beyond must be continuously considered.

- People want a balanced life. While the golf course will continue to be a forum for developing business relationships, many other forums for individuals with diverse interests and fast-paced lives exist; individuals who want to get home to their family or work on their novel, or other passion. This requires a diagnostic attuning process of attending to one's own and the other's changing intentions and needs, and making decisions and choices accordingly.

Summary

In the first chapter, the tone has been set for attention to a relationship focus and the underlying guiding principles that we as authors bring to this writing. In the next chapter, the philosophical **Net***Being* foundation for a relationship focus is established. We offer five relationship characteristics, The Five R's, vital to deepening relationship satisfaction. In essence, it isn't just what you know intellectually, *it's what you feel*: knowing with your heart, mind, body, and soul.

Chapter 2 The Five R's of Relationship

In Chapter One, we established that there is a fundamental desire in all of us to be in relationship, and to develop relationships that flourish. The desire for relationship and developing deeper relationships is a basic and universal human need. This desire is a more popular subject today than at any other time in history. There are thousands of books written on relationships. Television shows talk about relationship. Individuals talk about relationship. Counselors, therapists, and success coaches talk about relationship. In spite of the interest and awareness, and an abundance of information about relationship, this greatest of all desires is largely unfulfilled. How can that be? Perhaps with all this information, we are still uncertain or confused about the vital factors that contribute to deepening relationship satisfaction.

Making the Choice

The process of choosing and deepening relationships is interrelated. At each point in your relationship, you and those to whom you relate may choose either to develop or not to develop your relationships further. How do we make that choice? Of course, there are many ways. One person described her experience as jumping belly first into the water. Jane describes her process. It's like going into a swimming pool and testing the water first. I gingerly test the water with toes, feet, and then slowly edge into the water. I temper my approach into the water with caution depending on whether it is a warm day in June versus a hot day in July. If the sun is shining or if it is overcast, I approach the water accordingly.

The same is true in relationship. We are continuously *feeling* our way along in the meeting with another. We test the temperature, gauging the mutuality and connection, and then step back to assess how it *feels*, and whether the other person or persons have a reciprocal response. A multitude of factors in our environment are considered in going forward. Sometimes, no holds barred, we jump right in!

We offer the following five R's to throw into the mix of discussion around this very critical topic: Rewardingness, Reciprocity, Rules, Resourcefulness, and Relation*shift.*

Rewardingness

Webster defines rewarding as *a sense of reward or worthwhile return.* We are building on this definition by defining **rewardingness** as *an ongoing exchange and flow based on mutual benefit for all.* This exchange may be in providing services or products, or sharing learning, contacts, or resources.

There exists a fundamental psychological principle that people are more likely to repeat behaviors that have rewarding consequences for them than those that do not. Relationships are likely to deepen if partners can increase the range and depth of the mutual rewards they receive from one another, and if they are able to sustain a high level of mutual trust and benefits.

The relationship provides joyful experiences. This is the reward itself!
Phil Black, a student, writer, and teacher of Gestalt Psychotherapy poses the rhetorical question *"…when all goals are close to equal, what determines who we remain in relationship with whether it is business or pleasure? It is the relationship itself that determines this decision-the ease and the pleasure derived. In the end, there must be joy: a laugh, a smile, or we will not find satisfaction, and we will not stay with or return to."*

Capturing his remark and adding, yes, it is the reward of the relationship that keeps us involved.

Reciprocity

Webster defines **reciprocity** as *a corresponding and complementary exchange:* the quality or state of being reciprocal. Through mutual dependence, action or influence, a mutual exchange of privileges takes place. This definition fits well with the underlying intention that is inherent to a relationship focus. Most long-standing relationships are grounded in some form of reciprocity in the giving and receiving of rewards.

Cunningham and Antill (1981) observe, *"It is indisputable that most human relationships are based on considerations of equity and exchange."* Sharing this view of reciprocity as a joint responsibility enhances and deepens the relationship and the connection.

Rules

Rules are defined by Webster's New World Dictionary as *an established regulation or guide for conduct.*

The definition for the purpose of this book is to reinforce that each of us brings rules to the relationship based on many personal factors *and* that rules also emerge in relationship. The personal factors, to name a few, may include personality characteristics, boundary preferences, time availability or urgency, level of experience, geographical or global factors, comfort level, life focus, or monetary needs/constraints. The rules that emerge are based on the reason for the relationship, the length of the relationship, the level of established trust, and the degree of confidence that exists. Rules constantly change as the relationship changes. While rules may become formal or contractual, rules are often informal. Relationship rules provide guidelines and clarify expectations for your own and your partner's interaction. Simply put, rules are the conditions for relationship. Remembering to look at these *rules* from time to time helps *uncover* whether the relationship rule continues to serve you well, or whether suspending or replacing the rule would serve the relationship better.

Resourcefulness

Webster defines resource as *a source of information or expertise; a source of supply or support.* **Resourcefulness** is *the ability to effectively and efficiently respond to problems and determines resources that are important (people, technology, materials, services, time, et cetera.)* Resourcefully, responding to the need in the moment calls for attention to ongoing and emerging needs. This constant reevaluation help answer the question *what is needed now.* The ongoing accumulation of knowledge and skills help you become more and more resourceful in relationships. Further, resourcefulness helps in the taking of a large network of contacts into purposeful *connections.*

Relation*shift*

The spirit of the word **relation*shift*** reflects that a relationship never really ends, it simply flows to something else. Through a relation*shift*, the relationship becomes relevant or figural again when time, opportunity and a mutual focus reemerges. The concept of relevance further expands the definition to consider the questions who, why, when, where, and how. We have changing needs and we need to ask a host of questions as we go forward in relationship. Paying attention to relevance in a given situation keeps an "on-target" focus toward developing that which currently aligns to what is most important to self and the other. In short, *relevance* is constantly changing. That is the very reason attention to the *shift* taking place in relationship is important.

> **The process of recognizing the transformation of a relationship to something else is one of the most *liberating* realizations an individual can experience: freeing self up to letting go and moving on while *recreating* a relationship vision with *the same person.* In one's personal and professional life this allows for a natural transformation of relationship.**
>
> *- Jane*

While the relevance of the relationship is changing *in the present,* it is also imperative for all of us to understand that relationships, as a whole, always have been and always will be shifting! A collaboration ending now, may come back again twenty years from now. Relevance reemerges, if you will, around a common goal. Developing a meaningful and quality relationship is the lifeblood of taking your personal and professional relationships to the next level--lifting up and helping others along the way. When we look at a relationship with these eyes, we see that we can easily pick up again as we move forward in our personal and professional life.

Summary

The five relationship factors presented in this chapter are foundational to taking your personal and professional relationships to the next level. The 5 R's, rewardingness, reciprocity, rules, resourcefulness, and relation*shift,* support a relationship focus whereby new possibilities are continuously created. Each of these factors describes a context for the existence, the fluidity, the vitality, and the richness of the relationship to emerge and flourish. The 5 R's reinforce the importance of paying attention to the relationship based on benefits, common interests, resource identification, expectations, requirements, and mutuality.

The next chapter describes how networking and relationship building has changed over the years. The chapter further expands on the philosophy of **Net***Being,* describes the current reality and why it is essential to develop relationship skills and discover the abundant opportunities that are possible in relationship.

Net*Being*

Taking your Personal & Professional Relationships to the NextLevel

Chapter 3

The previous chapter presented five relationship factors. In this chapter we are looking at the history of networking to further establish the underpinnings for **Net***Being,* while clarifying the distinction between networking and **Net***Being.* Historical perspective will provide insight and move us forward toward this new paradigm. In short, knowing where we've been helps us know where we are going and why.

Let's take a moment and look at how networking has traveled over the years.

The 70s: It was all about how much *we* knew; an independent focus in creating our own success existed in the business community. We presented ourselves as experts and were less likely to share information for fear of losing our ideas, our competitive advantage, or our share in the market place.

The 80s: How much we knew and *who* we knew. We developed our ability to negotiate and compete, and still believed we were independently creating our own success.

The 90s: Who we could gain access to. We looked at six degrees of separation, and all the ways we could *reach* and *develop* a business network. We also began to see, with the explosion of the quality movement, information sharing, involvement, and a more global market calling for establishing solid networks of relationships. The philosophy of networking exploded within the business community.

The 2000s: **Net***Being,* a new intelligence of relationship building, adds to our learning from the 1990s on *how well* we are able to respond to the needs of individuals. When we are continuously paying *attention* to individuals, we can better help them. This new intelligence includes more than responding to the obvious task or project efficiently and effectively. It is also about *how* enjoyment is derived in the process. Most importantly, going forward is about *deepening* relationships and *attending* to a multitude of ever changing factors.

To further capture the distinction, consider the following:

- It's a place we are coming from, as opposed to a place we are going to.
- It's a way we are all the time and everywhere, as opposed to something we do some times and some places.
- It brings the whole person to the forefront of every interaction.
- It supports the very familiar rule of reciprocity: what goes around comes around.
- It balances and integrates autonomy and interdependence.

The following further highlights the distinction between networking and Net*Being*.

Networking		Net*Being*	
Distinction	**Benefits/Limitations**	**Distinction**	**Benefits**
A place you go	Event Oriented	A place you are coming from	Life Changing and Inspiring
Something you do sometimes and some places.	Situational and Sporadic	Something you do all the time and everywhere.	Focused
Meet with others to achieve individual goals.	Independence Oriented	Meet with others to build collaborative goals.	Interdependence Oriented
Seeks to make contacts.	Quantity Focused	Understands how to convert contacts to connections	Quality Focused and Creative
Support is individually focused.	Limited Mentality	Support is a collaborative process.	Abundance Mentality; Opportunity Abounds
Personal satisfaction	How can I achieve my dreams?	Mutual satisfaction and dream fulfillment.	How can we both achieve our dreams?
Transactional Relationship concludes.	Short Term Transaction is over	Purposeful Relationship shifts	Long Term Relationship evolves to another relationship

> **Net***Being*, now and beyond, is an overlapping of individual *purposes.* It moves creativity, resources, and ideas toward a mutually supportive, rewarding, and *purposeful* relationship.

A changing world has narrowed the boundaries *of the world* and opened up opportunities that two short decades ago would not have been imagined. A Fast-paced economy calls for interfacing with others in multifaceted ways, and our relationship web now extends throughout the world. Therefore, the 21st century provides unique opportunities and *challenges* in building business and personal relationships. **Net***Being* focuses the state of concentration on meeting challenges with greater and greater ease.

In addition to the many challenges we faced in previous decades, the following factors now face us as well:

- The information age bombards us with hundreds if not thousands of messages and bits of information every day. We must stay abreast of what is important and stay tuned in to changing trends. Now, in reaction to almost instantaneous information from all over the world, a *chain reaction of change* is perpetuating an ever-revolving *change reaction.*

- Quality of life considerations and the diversity of our times challenge us to pay attention to how we approach business relationships. Family and life balance issues have always been critical issues for most people. Now, more and more individuals are making decisions based on that which is most important to them.

- With today's technological revolution there are virtual offices everywhere. Telecommuting, videophones, video conferencing, black board conferencing, teleconferencing, emailing, faxes and modems, cellular phones and laptops give us unprecedented access all over the world.

- How we think about work is changing. There is an old joke about two manufacturing employees. The first worker asks: "Is your job in jeopardy?" The second worker responds: "No, my job is very secure. It's me they can do without." More and more individuals are becoming entrepreneurs, both in response to their desire to navigate their own destiny, and from reengineering, downsizing, and rightsizing that has occurred within their organizations. These new entrepreneurs are looking at each other for markets, for resources, for products, for services, and for business relationships.The new reality will continue to challenge how we think about work as mergers and acquisitions and a leaner flatter organization continues to evolve.

- To keep up with the changing world, knowing how to access knowledge and information is vital. Think about that. The world is changing; yesterday's knowledge base is not enough to carry you forward. In fact, new information and technology are advancing so rapidly that you literally cannot keep up. You must learn how to obtain the information you need. The beauty of this revolution of need matching up with technology is that *just-in-time-knowledge* (JIT-K) is only a fingertip away. A JIT-K perspective helps to prevent information overload and apply the knowledge as needed. Some may call this wisdom!

When we fundamentally understand that we have a multitude of considerations that impact how we are in relationship, our view of change and the importance of change is magnified. Consider Ron's personal view of change.

Let's take a few minutes and communicate about relationships and change. When you were a youngster, did you enjoy looking into a Kaleidoscope? Were you amazed at the infinite varieties of colors and patterns that evolved as it turned in your hand? Did you ever turn it so quickly that you did not have a chance to fully appreciate what you were watching because things were changing so quickly in the little viewer?

Net*Being* is not a place you are going to but a place you are coming from.

The world of relationship is like a Kaleidoscope. The changes in the viewer pale in comparison to the changes experienced in the last decade--and the changes we will experience in the years to come.

There was very little to think about when turning that little Kaleidoscope: just look and enjoy. If you view the world of relationship as a Kaleidoscope, you will see change. Rather than standing there mesmerized or memorizing the colors and patterns as if you can keep things the same, imagine what it might be like to be the colors. For openers, think about every second of your life, every minute, every day, being different from the preceding second, minute, or day. No two interactions or opportunities are the same, just as the patterns in the Kaleidoscope are never the same. Changes are inevitable--in behavior, in life patterns, in your knowledge base, in your habits, and in your relationships. We are not the same person we were even moments ago.

People change. Look around you. Are there new people in your life that were not there a month ago, six months ago, last year? Get to know people around you, and get involved with them. Don't just observe the changes passively, as if you are looking into a viewer. Be a part of them. Get to know people you come into contact with, what they do, what makes them tick. Become interested in them and how you can help them. They'll do the same for you and you'll enjoy life more.

Technology changes. Are you still using the same equipment as one, two, five years ago? Not very likely. And the equipment you are now using will become obsolete in the near future. Further more, staying abreast of the technological changes and discussing *preferred* communication tools with your partner is key in developing a collaborative relationship.

Leadership techniques change. When was the last time you picked up and read a management book for insight about new management and leadership practices?

An understanding of the changing needs of today's workforce (that's all of us!) will help you be more progressive and able to meet and partner with others within or outside your organization.

Economic factors, urgency, people's values, technology, and relationship management: all changing everyday, truly a Kaleidoscope. You can become a part of the Kaleidoscope--get inside the viewer--and be the one who determines the next pattern, if you make up your mind to. That's what the tools from this book will help you do.

Chapter 3

Summary

In this chapter, you have reviewed a historical perspective of how networking has changed. A new intelligence of **Net***Being* has been introduced--the intelligence of moving forward and building deeper relationships while considering the Kaleidoscope of ever changing dynamics in our world. **Net***Being* has been distinguished from networking recognizing that opportunity, creativity, and inspiration come in many forms. **Net***Being* calls for staying attuned to the *individual* and to the world business community, exposing the many possibilities along the way.

In the next chapter, we will discuss the desire for success, as you define success, and how developing a relationship focus is a crucial aspect of achieving that success.

Chapter 4 The Desire for Success

While the basic desire for success is naturally a part of all of us, what we view as important varies. A broad spectrum exists from improved health and fitness, greater personal development, achievement, travel, fulfilling relationships, a deeper spiritual life, a more harmonious family life, a more exciting social life, more financial freedom, education, personal growth, or more free time.

The desire for success hasn't changed over time; what's changed is our perception of the way we get there. We have always achieved success through relationship. Now we understand that to better help and receive help, we must fundamentally experience this in all aspects of our lives. Therefore, the *intention* to form solid relationships is at the forefront of all our interactions.

Many of us know this at a surface level. Bringing this principle to a heightened awareness propels us toward reaching out, tuning into the possibilities, the support, the creativity in relationship all around us. Jane provides an example about a relationship focus that helped her launch her business and continues to sustain her work.

When I started my consulting practice, Training and Development Resources, Inc., in 1996, I had many questions. How would I develop a client base? How would I market my business? How would I bring in other professionals when clients need a specialty that I am unable to offer?

After six months of planning before starting my practice, it was still with a leap of faith and many unanswered questions such as the ones above that I left the security of a Fortune 500 company in human resource management and development.

What I hadn't realized is that I had *unconsciously* developed business and networking relationships through volunteer work with the Chamber of Commerce, manufacturing and quality associations, and two association groups that I had co-founded.

Prior to having a marketing plan (I still don't have one), I confided in several people in my network that my intention was to utilize my experience and education and provide leadership training and development at all levels of the organization. I immediately had work! One individual asked me to make a proposal to his management team for supervisor development, and that proposal led to an immediate contract. The Chamber of Commerce asked me to lead a group on quality principles. I told them that I was not "ready" and they insisted that I was; after all, they had experienced me and developed a relationship with me. Ready or not, I began the work that I was called to and was calling me right back. From my initial workshops, my business has grown based on referrals, word of mouth, and, yes, relationships. Eight years later, my business continues: the result of the power of connection.

But that's not all! In a serendipitous lunch with racquetball friend and business acquaintance, Ron Sukenick, this co-writing opportunity was born and on the last day of 2002, our partnership launched on this writing project. This project has a life of its own, and will lead both of us to relationships that will lead to other relationships that will lead to other opportunities, and the matrix will continue to spiral and strengthen. The power of connection leading to connection leading to connection!

The driving force of this book is that relationships are primary to everyone's experience. We are constantly in relationship with our self, with others, and with a greater environment, world, and source. A continuous process of cultivating, attuning and attending to these relationships over a lifetime is part of the human experience we share with one another. Our observation skills, our diagnostic skills, and our remembering what is most important increases the quality of interaction in relationships, and, we would add, increases the quality of life.

Summary

The objective of this last chapter of Part One is to help you reflect on the importance of relationship to support each aspect of your life that you deem important.

In Part One, we have established the overall foundation for the reason behind paying attention to a relationship focus. First, we have presented that the desire for affiliation and relationship is central to all of us regardless of age, gender, or geography. Second, we defined *relationship* and identified five relationship factors that contribute to relationship success. Third, we established that each of us desires success, and uniquely define that success. Finally, we reinforce that we achieve that success in relationship through the support of others. We cannot achieve success on our own.

In Part Two, you will encounter fifteen relationship strategies to help you move toward success in all areas of your life. Relationship strategies are not contrived or phony gimmicks, or playing political games. In fact, these strategies are embedded within most of us already, and used in relationship everyday. Our intention is to bring them to the forefront as a basis for a deeper level of focusing, developing your talent for making connections, and for transforming how business and personal relationships are viewed and developed.

Whatever your situation may be, after reading this book we're hopeful that you will find relationship strategies valuable tools and an important part of achieving future success.

Strange is our situation here upon earth. Each of us comes for a short visit, not knowing why yet seeming to divine a purpose. From the standpoint of daily life there is one thing we do know. That we are here for the sake of others... Many times a day I realize how much my own outer and inner life is built upon the labors of others, both living and dead, and how earnestly I must exert myself in order to give in return as much as I have received and am still receiving.

Albert Einstein

PART TWO

Chapter 5 The Fifteen Strategies at a Glance

Welcome to the second part of the book where we uncover the 15 relationship strategies.

Why use the word strategy? Think of strategy as a plan of action, put in place to achieve specific objectives. Simply defined, a relationship strategy is a purposeful focus relating to the delivery of value to another person. While most people recognize the importance of strategy, relatively few actively develop a *formal* strategy with the notion of relationship in mind. After you spend time with this book, you will have increased your relationship awareness and diagnostic skills of strategies for a given situation.

Here is an overview of fifteen strategies that will move you closer to creating the relationships you envision.

Strategy One
Live Life Purposefully:
The Relationship Within

Personal awareness and self-knowledge emerge out of self-reflection. Through this knowledge, you clarify your intentions for your life! What is the fire within you that is unique to *you?* Once you see your life purpose more clearly, you will make more purposeful choices, and better see yourself, the person in front of you, and the opportunities that are possible together.

Strategy Two

Develop a Relationship Mindset:

Becoming a Relationship Builder

All experiences in life are the result of our predominant mental thought processes. Therefore, the key ingredient to this strategy is developing a relationship mindset to guide us forward. Engaging others with genuine sincerity and caring is essentially the most important aspect of relationship building. *It is something we do in the process of being mindful, something we are, and something we think.*

Strategy Three

Declare Your Interdependence & Cooperation:

Your Independence is a Direct Result

We are interdependent beings! We always have been and we always will be. All accomplishment, all satisfaction, all success, all progress that we as human beings have experienced has been based on our interdependence with others. When we truly embrace and *declare* this, we discover invisible and visible support systems all around us. This strategy focuses on this premise: from *interdependence* and *cooperation* comes even greater independence, self leadership, and self reliance.

Strategy Four

Listen Three Times as Much With Purpose:

Finding Joint Rhythm and Harmony

When you speak, you learn what you know. When you listen you learn what they know. To really hear someone, we must listen three times as much as we speak. When we listen three times as much with purpose, we bridge the gap for collaborating and creating together. Applying this strategy will help you become a more proactive listener and strengthen your communication foundation.

Strategy Five

Provide a Joyful Experience to Others:

Taking Relationships to the Next Level

Taking your relationships to the next level requires a *serious* commitment to a joyful process. In your interaction with others, bringing out who they are as a person is one way to provide a joyful experience. Bringing creativity into play will energize all parties and take both of you to a new and exciting level. This strategy is all about helping you think about how you might provide joy to another.

Strategy Six

Consistently Doing the Little Things:

Make The Big Difference

The secret formula of doing the little things is founded on *attending* to the smallest of details. It may be as minute as a smile and a casual conversation, or sending an article that you believe the other person might be interested in. Perhaps you invite the individual to a business event. This strategy comes from the intelligence of attention, and the infinite ways you can make the big difference.

Strategy Seven

Create Unparalleled Visibility:

Learning to be Seen and Heard

Achieving and sustaining consistent visibility has always been and will always be at the forefront of all of your relationship efforts. This strategy focuses on the many ways you can multiply your efforts of creating visibility when constantly meeting new people, and exposing yourself to new and exciting possibilities.

Strategy Eight

Make the Connection:

Connecting the Dots

This strategy looks at the role of attention, awareness, time, and initiative in making connections. Supporting deep change in making connections, *intention* is the glue that helps connect the dots.

Strategy Nine

Travel at the Velocity of a Fast-Paced World:

Flowing at the Speed of Change

There is a dynamic process of change propelling us forward as we attend *within* the fast-paced world of change all around us. This strategy brings your attention to the biggest driving force in the world today: Speed in the face of change! Take a look at this strategy to gain a better understanding of how you can respond seamlessly, effectively, and efficiently, using velocity to support building solid relationships.

Strategy Ten

Shorten Learning Curves:

Move Into Dream Fulfillment

This strategy focuses on responding to the *momentum* of finding common ground quickly and effectively. Communicating your dreams, determining what to do together, and how to get things done follows beautifully. The cycle of interaction decreases and learning curves shorten, thereby increasing the opportunity to fulfill the dreams you and your business partner have for success.

Strategy Eleven

Move Into Legendary Status:

Going From the Ordinary to the Extraordinary

Commitment + Understanding + Relationship Passion = Shared Extraordinary Possibilities. This formula for relationship success provides a project management approach to move your relationship and your dream forward. This strategy will help propel your relationships into the extra ordinary.

Strategy Twelve
Become Technologically Savvy:
Building the Techno Advantage

This strategy delves into the vast technology available today. It emphasizes the importance of aligning with and learning the multitude of communication infrastructures at your fingertips. Breaking down the complexities of technology, you will create a framework for deciding which technology will best accomplish your objectives. This will help you choose the preferred communication medium to benefit the business partnership *in front of you.*

Strategy Thirteen
Become a Global Partner:
One World, One Playing Field

The future calls for taking on a more global understanding of the world around you. Facts, information, and knowledge are key ingredients. Tuning into the needs of others on a global level is intelligence beyond becoming smarter or working harder. Global partnerships are what this strategy is about.

Strategy Fourteen
Look Back to Move Forward:
Taking the Moment & Dancing With It

We have arrived at this point in time through the relationships that have come before. Our previous happiness and success directly correlate to being in relationship with another along the way to now. This strategy takes you back to consider the multitude of relationships possible to *reconnect* with reminding us that relationships never end. This strategy encourages you to ignite relationships by reconnecting, re-exploring, and reshaping previous connections.

Strategy Fifteen

Continuous Learning With Purpose:
Ongoing Enhancement of Life Through Personal & Professional Growth

Learning new skills, new ways of thinking, new technology, new business strategies, new information, new innovations, new management and leadership thought is a lifetime process. The lifelong learner is not only a survivor but embraces revival in all aspects of his or her life. This strategy caps off the fifteen strategies and provides a process for continuous learning: nourishing the heart, soul, and mind, and stimulating ongoing growth and development towards the best future.

Summary

Fifteen new tools for the relationship toolbox have been overviewed for you. Whatever you are thinking at this point…paying attention to the relationship is the first step toward better relationships.

Now, let's go on to the next chapter, where you will examine the first strategy, *Live Life Purposefully.*

> *If relationships are to be optimized, the human element of being in relationship must be recognized. Staying focused on who* ***we*** *are in relationship is truly transformative.*
>
> **Jane George-Surges and Ron Sukenick**

Chapter 6

Strategy One

Live Life Purposefully: *The Relationship Within*

> *He who conquers others is strong; he who conquers himself is mighty.*
>
> **Lao-tzu**

Jane: Martin Luther King gave his famous "I have a dream" speech in 1963. I was twelve years old and as I watched him on my family's black and white television set, I sat mesmerized by his passion. Like many of you, I have heard the speech many times since that day and thinking back, I can't say that I remember anything other than those four words "I have a dream." I would go to bed at night and before going to sleep, I would imagine what was possible for my life. These nightly rituals would start with "I have a dream." A year before graduating from Sisseton High School in Sisseton, South Dakota, I wrote my parents a *vision* letter, although I didn't call it that at the time. I told them about my job in Minneapolis and the job and life I had there. I wrote this letter as if I was already there. I imagined the life possible--a visioning process that stated in present tense the life I saw for myself a year ahead. That vision didn't come to fruition the way I had planned. I did move to Minneapolis and later that summer, married my high school sweetheart. Life took many twists and turns but dreaming and creating a vision for possible futures remained constant.

What took me awhile to become aware of was *coming from purpose.* What is the purpose of my life unique to me? I stayed with that question until it revealed itself! Once my purpose was revealed, I became much more focused in all aspects of my life. I had a touchstone in which to take those dreams, those visions, those intentions for my life forward. This strategy is one process to help you reveal your purpose and to help you live life purposefully.

Chapter 6

The Foundation

Living life purposefully begins with identifying that which is uniquely *rare* to you. Find this rarity!

How do we find this rarity? Ron suggests that we go to school on ourselves. Look back through your life. Play a movie projector of those moments most significant to your gaining insight about yourself. Look at the shadows long forgotten. What is the common theme that has been there all along?

Another way to get to purpose is to begin with a question in mind and write as fast as you can for five minutes. *Suspend* thinking about the question. Simply pose it and then just allow the words to flow out of you. What this means is to simply write what comes into your consciousness. If nothing is coming, write *nothing is coming.* If what comes into consciousness is that *this is a silly exercise*...write this is a silly exercise. Carl Jung referred to this process as stream of consciousness. Trust the process and see what comes. Here are a few questions that have helped me and others. Feel free to identify your own questions.

The velocity of your life must slow down for purpose to be revealed.

1 What is your gift to the world?

2 Visualize yourself looking back at your life. How do you want your life to have been lived?

Once you have completed this writing, go back and circle the key words. Your purpose will be revealed not in the *doing* words but in the *being* words.

I have found that purpose can often *not* be stated to others. Purpose is often so personal, it can only be lived!

Consider your *life* purpose to be the foundation from which the rest of your life is built. This touchstone will guide you as you get ready, set, and take aim in all aspects of your life.

You are now ready to set intentions for your life, but before you do, let's talk about your unique career path that comes from your purpose.

A Unique Career Path

Once *purpose* is uncovered, you will be better able to *zoom* in on your career path or paths. What are the many ways that your purpose may be manifested through your work life? For Ron, most of his career life has been about making contacts and helping others network and make connections. He has done this through speaking, through writing, through coaching and through helping associations become more vibrant and capable of better supporting their members, and better market themselves. This comes directly out of his purpose which is to develop connections with others.

My purpose revealed is to develop myself holistically and to full potential. A central theme existed from my youth. People came along and told me their story, their struggles, their aspirations, and I provided the space for them to get quiet and determine for themselves what they were next drawn to do. My career life then was obvious. I was to help others develop holistically and to full potential! How perfectly aligned to my personal purpose! There are many ways that plays out for me: through teaching, through consulting to organizations, through leadership development, through life coaching, through speaking, and through my passion for writing.

Take a moment and think about your purpose again. How does your career life align to your purpose? Now go to the next section, and identify your life intentions, which include your career life.

Identifying Your Life Intentions

Living life purposefully continues with the current intentions you have for your life.

The intentions for all aspects of your life are often called life visions. These intentions establish the direction and paint the picture of where you would like to go. These intentions may include family, health, career, and life accomplishments.

Between the start and the outcome of the intentions for your life are clarity, leadership, accountability, and performance. Planning, goal setting, and action steps are the support structure to help you move forward.

Chapter 6

Planning: Goals & Objectives

Living life purposefully, *with your aim before you*, is not alone a matter of skill, ability, knowledge, or effort. It is additionally a matter of identifying your goals and objectives that stem from your purpose and intentions.

As you move toward your goals and objectives, consider the following:

Are current goals and objectives in line with intentions? If they align you then have the incomparable edge to accomplish what you *intend* to achieve. Your goals and objectives will help you identify and then attract people, partnerships, and resources to help you.

The final stage of planning is identifying action steps and assigning time frames for their completion. Taking action steps *now*, small and large, toward goals and objectives that may be six months or ten, twenty, or thirty years away will help you move incrementally toward these objectives. Take a moment now to reflect on the following model that supports this strategy. Make it real through your action and commitment.

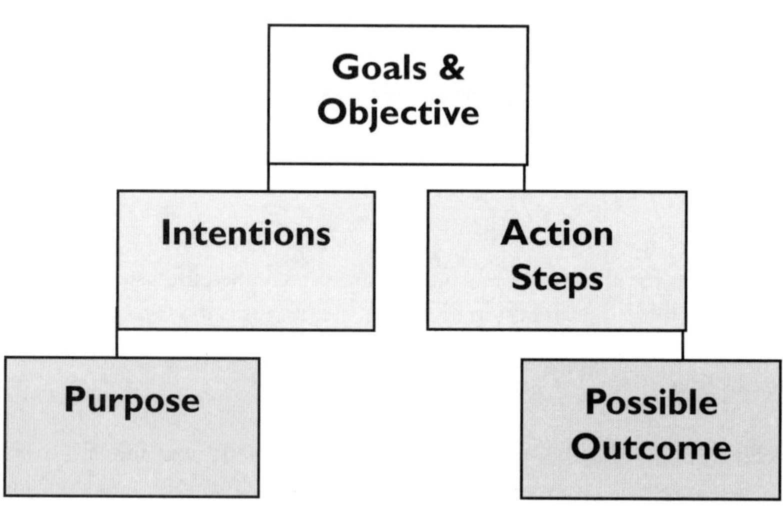

The Dynamics of Clarity

Have you ever noticed reaching a sense of calm and peace, that "still place within," when only moments before you were filled with anxiety or uncertainty? How do you find that sense of peace when previously you were filled with angst? Probably you took a step back, created a questioning pause, and reflected on a guiding principle for your life. You may have asked yourself the question, "Which decision most aligns with my life purpose and my intentions?" The answer comes quite quickly through the process of discernment, and so does a sense of calm, peace, and clarity.

Once you become clear about what you are aiming for in your personal and professional life, you become clear about three things: 1.) How to spend your time. 2.) Which relationships are important to you, and 3.) What action and activity align to the intention and vision you have for your life.

The Relationship Within

Purpose-filled living starts with personal clarity and focus. This focus guides you toward developing relationships that align what you *do* with *who* you are as you move toward a happy and satisfying life! The relationship within is learned in *contemplation* and by *action* in a world where people are continually discovering new ways of being, who are innovative and willing to take risks to discover new possibilities, and who continuously learn about self in relationship with others. We must go within to discover this clarity.

Internal Contents

To live *purposefully*, we ask you to learn as much about yourself as possible. Looking inward helps you find hidden gifts and motivations, as well as unknown resistances, blocks, and "stuck" behaviors that may be holding you back. The internal life contains the jewels: good, bad, or ugly, that influence how you live and choose your life.

When you start within, you are better able to flow in the world with others. You choose your outer life--how you will "show up" in life, respond to situations, and your overall outlook and world view. You better choose your career and relationships that support a purpose filled life.

Thinking Points for Connecting Forward

- Are you reflecting your purpose and intentions for your life through your daily life and choices?
- Are you listening to what your inner self is telling you about a choiceful life?
- Are you increasing your awareness of how goals, objectives, and action steps align to a purposeful life?
- Are you identifying internal thoughts that get in the way of living the life you want for yourself?
- How are you embracing this magnificent journey that is your life?

Summary

Living life purposefully comes from knowing that which is most important to you, and possessing self-discipline as you make sound choices for your personal and professional life. In this first strategy you have reflected on identifying your purpose: the touchstone for you to return to time and time again as you live life forward. You have also identified intentions for yourself that reflect the whole of your life. Planning and goal setting are tools that will help you create the future you desire for yourself. You have been encouraged to think about your internal contents that help you or get in your way. In Part Three of this book, you will find a framework to further put into action this most important strategy.

As you face unpredictable outcomes, this strategy and process will help you stay on a purposeful course when the solutions are uncertain and the answers are unknown.

Ron and I began this section with a quote by Johann Wolfgang von Goethe. In the sixth line of this passage, Goethe writes *"Boldness has genius, power and magic in it."* Purpose begins with self discovery, introspection and clarity.

Now that you have revalidated your purpose or have gotten clear for the first time and you have clarified what is most important to you through your intentions, set goals and objectives, begin, begin, begin! Begin it now.

In the next chapter, you will devote your attention to strengthening your ability to develop a relationship mindset engaging others with genuine sincerity and caring.

> *...almost anybody can learn to think or believe or know, but not a single human being can be taught to be.*
>
> **e. e. cummings**

Chapter 7

Strategy Two
Develop a Relationship Mindset: *Becoming a Relationship Builder*

> *The most important single discovery of this generation is that we change our conditions by changing our attitude of mind.*
>
> **William James**

Ron: A turning point in developing my relationship mindset occurred about twenty years ago. I was on a plane from L.A to N.Y. to visit my parents. It was one of those midnight specials. The plane wasn't as full as I am sure the airline wished it would have been, and the opportunity to stretch out across the entire row of seats made itself available.

What happened next I believe literally changed my life, or, at least my *attitude* about life and the power behind developing a relationship building mindset.

On awakening after a few undisturbed hours of restful sleep, I felt something at my head. Grabbing to feel what it was, I picked up this 5 x 7 black-covered book titled *The Master Key System* by Charles Haanel. For whatever reason, somebody either accidentally dropped it at my head, or possibly placed it there for me to enjoy for the rest of my life.

Let's take a moment to examine some of Charles Haanel's ideas. The book points out that *much gathers more* is true on every plane of existence, and that *loss leading to greater loss* is equally true. Our minds are creative, and conditions, environment and all experiences in life are the result of our *habitual* or predominant mental *attitude.*

Our attitude of mind depends upon what we think. Therefore, *the secret of all power, all achievement, and all possibility* depends upon our *thinking.*

This is true because we must "BE" before we can "DO," and we can "DO" only to the extent which we "ARE," and what we "ARE" depends upon what we think.

Our *attitude of mind* toward life pretty much determines the experiences with which we are to meet. If we expect nothing, we shall have nothing; if we expect much, we shall receive the greater portion.

The important aspect of this strategy is recognizing how our thoughts are getting in the way, and focusing on relationship connecting, rather than spending our energy on negative thoughts about the relationship or the individual, or what is not working. We are able to focus on gathering more.

Relationship Networks

Jane: Intangible elements are vital to building successful relationships. Successful relationship means different things to different people. Listed below you will find four concentric rings reflecting the degree to which you move out into a larger network.

You Circle: You choose the level of relationship from a smaller inner circle, to a larger outer circle based on internal motivation.

Inner Circle: This is the level where your commitment, initiative, and interactions focus here first. While you may be interested in developing a larger relationship network, your "inner circle" is most vital. If you choose to not go out from here, it could reflect that you're really not interested in doing any more, or you are not sure how to expand outward. You may be focusing on relationships closer to you, and/or prefer a smaller network. Life span decisions and personal reflections may be taking you from outer circles to a focus on relationships closer to you.

Middle Circle: This is where you focus on the interactions that support what you are currently doing. Overall, you are satisfied with your current state, and moderately increasing or stabilizing your personal and professional networks.

Larger Circle: Encompassing all circles, a relationship mindset is and has been a natural focus of your interactions. As is true for the inner and middle circle, you cheer others' successes forward, and constantly find ways to help wherever you can, even when it does not support your current doing. Your aim is to continually find ways to enhance the relationship, and expand your network of relationships for now and in the future.

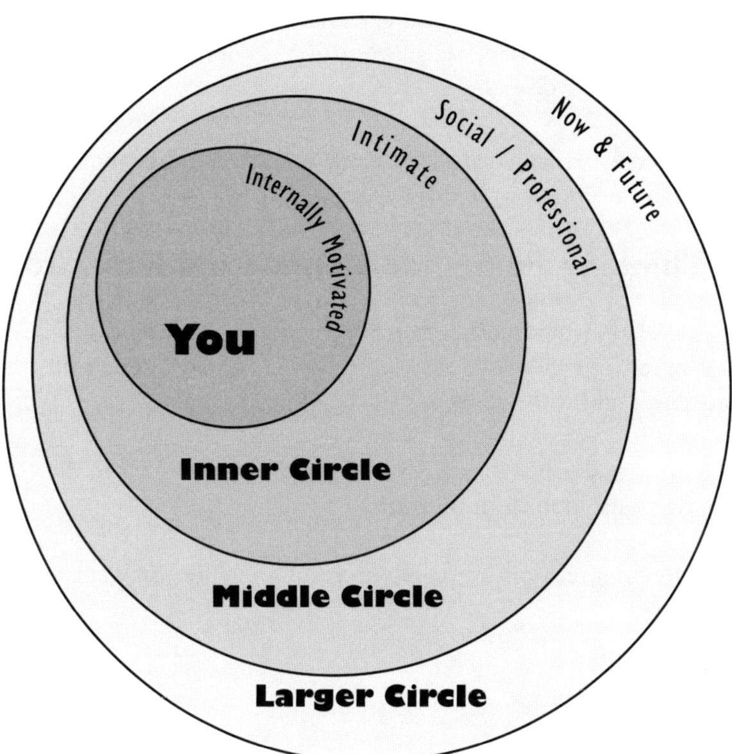

Commitment Within a Relationship Mindset

For many people, the biggest reward from commitment to the relationship process is that it leads to closer, warmer, and deepened relationships with others.

When you take a pro-active approach to developing relationship with others, others are eager to enter into business and social relationships with you. Now it doesn't mean that everybody will choose to interact with you. A relationship mindset simply increases the possibility that someone will *want* to interact with you!

> Develop a relationship mindset and with practice you will discover the ease of **Net***Being*.

Commitment is the foundation of this strategy. A relationship mindset begins with commitment and ends with commitment. Not only will you build strong relationships in your professional life with this commitment, but within your personal life as well. This strategy and the commitment that you develop, supports the passion behind the relationship process.

The difference between a successful relationship mindset and an unsuccessful relationship mindset is *attitude.*

Thinking Points for Connecting Forward

- A relationship mindset calls for a state of mindfulness: a quieting of our thoughts allowing us to be more present with ourselves and with others
- Are you living your life forward mindfully attending to the relationship in front of you?
- How is a relationship mindset creating the life you want to be living?

Summary

This strategy has emphasized the importance of fostering an *attitude of mind* toward building solid long lasting relationships with others. We have also focused on the foundational principle of *commitment* to a relationship mindset, providing descriptions to help you diagnose where you are and where you would like to be. In closing, a relationship mindset supports the relationship process in a positive and enduring way. In Part Three, you will find an assessment for you to gauge your current level, and ways to build and maintain this skill.

Now, straight ahead is Strategy Three: Declare Your Interdependence. If you haven't before, you will truly see that all success, all individual success, is inherent to fully engaging in this very interdependent world that we live in.

> *It's a relationship attitude that supports the relationship building process in a positive and enduring way.*
>
> **Ron Sukenick**

Strategy Three

Declare your Interdependence & Cooperation: *Your Independence is a Direct Result*

Chapter 8

> *Known to the wise, Abraham, Buddha, Confucius, and Jesus understood the underlying connectedness of all humanity. Their admonitions to us contain high awareness of our human interdependence.*
>
> **Timothy Wilken**

Jane: All accomplishment, all achievement, all success, all progress that we as human beings have experienced is a result of our *interdependence* with others! A tremendous amount of support surrounds us in all areas of our lives; our families, our friends, our business colleagues, our partnerships, our educators, our children, our community, our state, our country, our world are *visible* support structures.

While the list of this interdependent support goes on, as individuals we often fail to realize that *independence* is a direct result of our interdependence and cooperation with others. We cannot truly become independent without the help of others! How do we achieve independence? We must learn to ask for this help! Independence is achieved through interdependent associations when people are united together to support each other: mentoring, coaching, sharing resources and referrals, working together toward common objectives, and helping in numerous ways. There are endless examples of how our interdependence affects each of us every day. While for many of us there is a higher force providing invisible support, Ron will provide examples of invisible support from our everyday environment.

Ron: Here are obvious *invisible* examples of our interdependence. Before we wake up in the morning, there's someone at the electric company making sure our lights will go on when we flip the switch. The water company pumps and stores water waiting for our beckoning call at the faucet. Farmers and truckers are growing and transporting food products to our local grocer who in turn, makes these products available to our community, our families and to us. Oil companies are drilling oil from around the world and shipping the oil to our neighborhoods allowing us the freedom to drive our cars when and where we choose.

There are countless more examples that demonstrate that almost every action we take throughout our day has *visible* and *invisible* support structures of interdependent relationships.

Dr. Wolf Rinke, a management consultant and author shares a story about the impact of one relationship that really opens our eyes to understanding the power of interdependence.

About eight years ago I was delivering a seminar at Langkawi Island, Malaysia. Afterwards a woman, who was the human resource director for a global import-export company headquartered in Singapore, introduced herself and asked if I would have lunch with her. We struck up a conversation and found that we had lots in common. We were both from Europe, she was Danish and I was originally from Germany, and we hit it off real well. After that we kept in touch and about three months later she began hiring me to conduct numerous executive development programs for her leadership team all over the Pacific Rim. Over the span of about three years I conducted more than 20 seminars, and provided a variety of management consulting and executive coaching sessions for her.

After she left that company she moved to Australia to pursue a graduate degree, where she continued to live for several years. Again we kept in touch. I was there for her whenever she needed an "electronic keyboard to cry-on" or when she needed the advice of a friend and mentor. We maintained this virtual relationship for about two years when one day I received an e-mail from her telling me that she is now on the HR team of the second largest Danish company-a global company with over 700,000 employees world-wide. She further states that they are in the process of setting up a corporate university, and she would like me to help. Since then I have traveled at least four times to Copenhagen to conduct full day leadership development programs for executives from all over the world. And I have been doing that now for just about three years. All of that business from just one relationship. Need I say more?

Making the Point

Jane: As Dr. Rinke describes, one relationship can propel us forward in unimaginable ways, greatly impacting our opportunities, possibilities, and satisfaction. For both Dr. Rinke and the woman he describes, what was central was a mutually rewarding connection personally and professionally, where their interdependence supported both of them.

Think of times when you may not have recognized or had a support system in place. How did you function? How did you do personally and professionally? Possibly not so well. Now think of another time. Perhaps five, ten, or thirty years ago with the help of one person, you chose another path that has led you to the independent and satisfying life you now lead. In interdependent relationships, tremendous learning, support, performance and opportunities become exponentially possible.

Understanding this keeps us mindful of continually developing interdependence for ourselves and recognizing our contributions to the success and potential of another. As part of a larger interdependent world, we have the continued opportunity to receive and give back, becoming liberated and independent contributing to liberation and independence for others.

One of the central features of relationships then is our awareness of interdependence. We move from seeing ourselves as separate from one another, to seeing ourselves as connected and interdependent with one another.

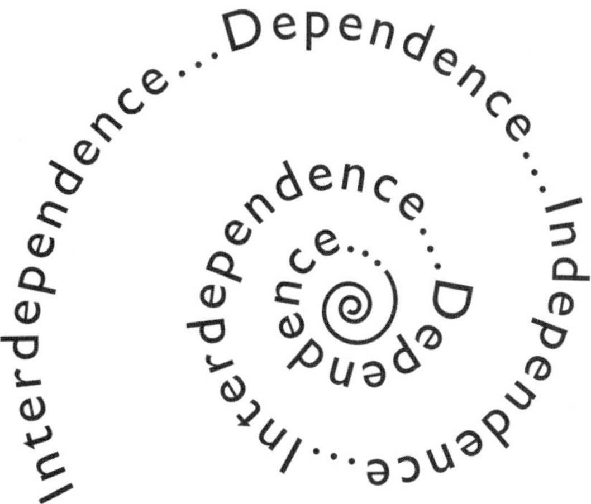

A process of *interdependence* allows us, as individuals to be STRONG enough to be dependent when new behaviors, new skills, and new learning are required. When we are able to do this in an interdependent world, we move toward independence and self-reliance.

When *interdependent* behavior is high, individuals are making connections continuously, providing help and asking for help. Individuals are connecting others to others and, therefore, strengthening connections in a web of relationship that far exceeds you and me.

When *independent* behavior is high, individuals are focusing on their individual success and are more apt to be self sufficient and self-reliant. *Overly* independent, individuals may not make the connections they need to continue to grow personally and professionally or to contribute to the success of others.

When interdependence is practiced and embraced, independence is a natural product. Individuals are able to get needed support and better move in relationship with the world. Recognizing that there is a time for *dependence* allows us to move to full potential by first suspending our independence. For many of us, this is a very vulnerable place. Becoming vulnerable in all aspects of our lives will help us ask for the help we need, and to better move easily in and out of relationship as we develop new and untested processes.

Fostering an interdependent environment creates an incredible web of support that is transformative to one's life and to the world!

Interdependence Unleashed

Ron: Consider this three-part process that moves us more deeply into strengthening interdependent relationships.

Interdependence + Cooperation = Cooperative Relating

Cooperative relating is the integration of independence and cooperation. Mutual dependence takes place when we embrace this in our thinking and interactions: I need you and you need me. We act or work together, cooperating to achieve what both parties need/want. We own collectively, and share in the risks and the benefits, or experience the joy of helping another reach another level. In a truly cooperative relationship, this basic dynamic is extended repeatedly. Cooperative partners bring to light what is possible together.

Fostering an interdependent environment creates an incredible web of support that is transformative!

Thinking Points for Connecting Forward

- Think about the visible and invisible support structures that you have all around you.
- Think about the times in your life when you have felt most alone. When you made it through the challenge, what support from your environment assisted you?
- What support do you currently need to move you toward achieving the objective you have set for yourself?
- Life lessons come in relationship. What can you learn from those times when you didn't ask for help? What can you learn from those times you did ask for help?

Summary

This strategy helps reinforce the awareness that we do not come to any situation alone. We never have, and we never will. *Visible* and *invisible* support systems are all around us. We help others and we are helped by others. Understanding this, we are better able to look at each other in a way that is relational, experience joy and satisfaction, identify what we need in a given situation, and better help and support another. We see how our interdependence strengthens the ability to be independent. Interdependence ultimately results in liberation: the ability to be self sufficient, and to contribute to the world. The next strategy will help you focus your attention and intention on *purposeful* listening with heart and mind.

Fully recognizing that we are interdependent beings reinforces the fundamental and enduring principle that we know at our core that we are not alone in our living, never have been, and never will be.

Jane George-Surges

Chapter 9

Strategy Four
Listen Three Times as Much with Purpose: *Finding Joint Rhythm & Harmony*

> *Listening effectively to others can be the most fundamental and powerful communication tool of all. When someone is willing to stop talking or thinking and begin truly listening to others, all of their interactions become easier, and communication problems are all but eliminated.*
>
> **Ken Johnson**

Ron: Here I am turning fifty-four and I still feel I can get better in building the kind of relationships I desire. And while I've heard over the years how important listening is to the relationship building process, today, more than ever, I've come to learn how true that is.

I remember one day attending the National Speakers' Association conference in Atlanta, Georgia. Think about it: 2,000 professional speakers and everyone running around speaking…but who was there to listen? Kind of makes you laugh, doesn't it?

Then, all of a sudden, it came to me…*listening with purpose,* if better understood, and better utilized could help to reap more of the rewards we all look for.

Let's take a few moments to define purposeful listening. Purposeful listening is listening with your five senses (smell, touch, taste, hearing, and sight), and with your heart, mind, and soul. Through purposeful listening, you make good contact with the other, and the other truly feels heard. Through listening, you may give a person an opportunity to work through an issue he or she is struggling with, or hear an experience he or she wants to tell you about. Or, you listen to hear how you might partner on a project together, finding a way to become more useful and resourceful to him or her.

Who would ever think that becoming a great listener is a way of being useful and resourceful to others?

Let us take you back a few years to grade school. Remember the three R's? Wasn't it reading, writing, and arithmetic? When do you last recall hearing of anybody taking a listening course in the early formative years of our education? In fact, how many listening courses do they offer in high school or even at the college level now? You probably won't be able to find many. Maybe if you're lucky, you'll find a course offered in a continuing educational forum at one of your local colleges.

Yet, the *power* of all knowledge and the *power* that's available to build the relationships we desire are in our *increased* and dramatically *improved* ability to listen with purpose to what people are saying, and most of all, discover what they really mean.

Your ability to listen to the needs of others is one of the most important relationship skills. It's often been said that we have two ears and one mouth and that we should listen proportionally. If you agree with this basic concept, and if you are willing to take your listening efforts to the next level, listen three times as much with *purpose.*

When Does Failure to Listen Occur?

Failure to listen occurs whenever the receiver "tunes out" the sender of the message before receiving the entire message. One instance is when you disagree with some part of what is being said; you listen to the point of disagreement, and begin formulating your response in your head rather than continuing to listen.

This is the old habit of listening to only what you want to hear and failing to listen to the rest of the message. As a result, the message is misunderstood and not heard.

Here are two quick exercises that will help you understand this principle:

1 Place a clean sheet of paper in front of you

2 Now spell out two words from these letters using all of them:

O O D R W W T S

Are you done? Still working on it?

OK, you can now look at the bottom of the page and see the answer to this problem.

Now what did this teach you about the need to listen (read) carefully? What did this teach you about the need to look for meaningful patterns in the clues given by others? Now let's try just one more.

Are you hearing what I just said?

Take 30, divide by half, add ten, the answer is? Let me ask you one more time. Take 30 divide by half add ten the answer is? Now for those of you who answered twenty-five that's the correct answer but to a different question. You see if I said take 30 and divide by two that would be fifteen and then if you added ten, the answer would be twenty-five. But if you remember correctly, I suggested that you take 30 and that you divide by half. Half goes into 30, 60 times and when you add 10, the answer is 70.Our intention is not to present a tricky question; our intention is to make a point. You see, many of us respond quickly to the questions that we think are being asked. We don't hear what is said. By doing so, we miss the real question, and the opportunity to respond with understanding and knowledge.

Answer: "Two Words"

When we find ourselves not listening to others it's often a product of being bored, tired, hurried, or a dozen of other reasons that we come up with. Who cares what the reason is? The fact is, we *assume* we hear. In any event, we are *not* purposeful in our listening efforts. To become a more purposeful listener, we first commit to listening, assuring that we indeed did hear the words that the person expressed. We then ask questions and put into our own words to clarify that we *understand* what the other person is saying. The light bulb pretty quickly goes on when we find that we have truly heard and truly do understand another. This kind of listening helps reveal deeper feelings and needs.

To hear is to hear with our heart.

Let's continue to look at developing listening skills.

Development of Listening Skills

Jane: When we listen with purpose, we profoundly transform ordinary conversation to deeper dialogue where we are better able to create together.

The attentive listening process encompasses skills that strengthen our ability to choose language and use inquiry to assist in encouraging the other to speak openly.

Here is an example of listening three times as much on the way to finding joint rhythm and harmony:

Shortly after John, a financial planner had attended a workshop on listening three times as much, he met Mark at a business conference. Over lunch they learned that they had similar backgrounds in accounting and financial planning. John, in banking, and Mark in manufacturing. Further, they learned they were both interested in starting their own businesses. John was excited by the meeting and that same week emailed Mark to tell him he had several ideas about joint ventures and was eager to explore possibilities with Mark.

John and Mark met on Friday at a quiet coffee house. They barely sat down with their coffees in hand when the following transpired between them:

Mark: *John, I hear your excitement, and while I'm also excited, I need to slow down this process. While I'm open to leaving the security of my position, I need to be very careful that I also pay attention to the financial needs of my family.*

John: *Mark, tell me more and then I'll share my situation as well.*

(This helps create a pause and is the first stage of purposeful listening. John has established that he has heard Mark, and encourages Mark to share more. It also creates a sense of mutuality and safety in that Mark is assured that John will share his situation.)

Mark: *I have been with my organization for ten years, and it supports my wife and three kids, our monthly mortgage, and car payment. On the other hand, I strongly believe that there's a better life in the possibility of owning my own business.*

John: *It sounds like you'd like to leave your organization but the benefits and compensation are pretty important to you at this point in time. Is that correct?*

(This demonstrates purposeful listening whereby John puts into his own words what he is hearing, and asks for Mark to respond yes or no. Overall, it helps to encourage Mark to go forward. This demonstrates the second stage of purposeful listening.)

Mark: *Yes, I don't want to mislead you that I am able to take a financial risk at this point.*

John: *Thanks, Mark. We're both in our mid 30's and I, too, am raising a family. A financial base is important to me also.*

(This exchange continues the second stage of purposeful listening and clarifies the issue that is most important to Mark. It also demonstrates that they indeed do have a common base. If not, John might reply that he is at a point where he can take a bigger risk, and that they may not share this fundamental common ground at this point. There may be other avenues also that are possible to explore at this point. What is key here is that they both understand the issue that is central.)

Mark: *That's a relief, John. From our conversation the other day, I knew we had complementary skills, but I wasn't sure that we had a shared view around the financial security piece.*

John: *I also like knowing that any partner I have feels a similar commitment to financial security. If, in our exploration, we keep the financial security as a must, do you feel we could continue to brainstorm possibilities?*

(This is the final stage of listening three times as much. Mark is now given the opportunity to state any final concerns and/or agree to go forward.)

Mark: *Absolutely and frankly, I'm relieved. I've been wanting to go out on my own for some time but the financial piece has always prevented me from exploring any further. If we agree that we pay attention to minimal financial risk, I think we can begin the brainstorming you mentioned.*

John: *I agree! Let's begin and, hopefully, we can continue to be as candid as you just were.*

(At this point John reinforces that this listening process is important to their continued success in communication. Mark and John have set the foundation for purposeful listening, finding joint rhythm and harmony. If they continue this process, they will be able to work together toward creating something profound together, and address key issues and concerns as they go forward.)

Listen Three Times as Much

1. Personally pause and commit to purposeful listening.
2. Ask questions and put into your own words, clarifying that you understand the other's intention.
3. Respond final understanding by once again using your own words and asking "is this it?" When the individual indicates "yes, you've heard me," you have completed the final stage of listening three times as much with purpose. If you haven't already established where you are as it pertains to the topic at hand, you now ask the individual if this is a good time for them to hear your thinking and feelings on the matter. You have just modeled the process so most will have little trouble listening to you as well.

4 Once there is common understanding, you have achieved joint rhythm and harmony, and are ready to move on in the communication process.

Your ability to listen attentively to others is the beginning of finding harmony and joint rhythm toward this connection. Trust is a fantastic byproduct. We are more inclined to trust others when they truly hear us, and the opposite is also true.

Great listeners have great connections.

Purposeful Communication and Resistance to Changing The Communication Process

We are all resistant at times to change! When you feel this resistance rise up in you, pause and look behind the resistance. Are you giving up the comfortableness of a proven communication success and going into unknown territory? Are you moving from your current capability of talking about the weather, what you do for a living, about the project at hand, et cetera? There's nothing wrong with that. In fact, sharing common experiences early in an interaction will help everyone feel comfortable. Taking the next step may feel vulnerable and awkward. One way to practice this is to talk about what you are feeling, what you are aware of in the moment. Simply notice and remember with practice, deepening the person-to-person connection will become natural.

Jane

Thinking Points for Connecting Forward

- Your ability to listen attentively to others is the beginning of facilitating a deeper connection.
- Is there someone you are currently experiencing a disconnect with? How might listening help you better understand and reconnect with this person?
- We are more inclined to trust others when they truly hear us, and the opposite is also true.

Summary

The successful implementation of this strategy is based on understanding the importance of purposeful listening. Through the listening process, we, *you and I*, find our rhythm and our harmony together. Listening three times as much provides the following opportunities: you get more from the interaction, you affirm the person or persons you are listening to, your understanding of the message is greatly enhanced, and you lay the foundation for increased cooperation and collaboration.

Strategy Five is straight ahead! Providing a Joyful Experience to Others: Taking Relationships to the Next Level provides a context for deepening relationships and **Net***Being* experiences.

> *History repeats itself because no one listens the first time.*
>
> **Lynn White, Jr.**

Chapter 10 Strategy Five
Providing a Joyful Experience to Others: *Taking Relationships to the Next Level*

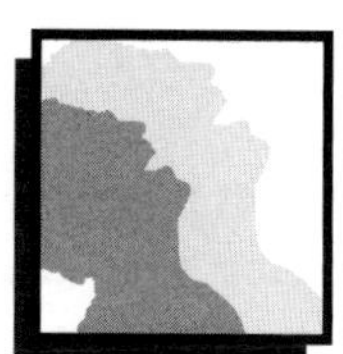

Too often we underestimate the power of a touch, a smile, a kind word, a listening ear, an honest compliment, or the smallest act of caring, all of which have the potential to turn a life around.

Leo Buscaglia

Ron: In my first book, *Networking Your Way to Success,* I addressed nine networking strategies. One of those strategies was act like a host, never a guest. Let's expand on that strategy and explore the real power of providing a joyful experience to others.

The word Joy comes from the Latin word *gaudium,* meaning "pleasure, gladness and happiness." Its inherent nature is one of sudden surprise. Joy also shows many sides and arises as a result of both internal and external stimuli. Joy is both a physical sensation and an emotional feeling. When we experience Joy, we feel complete and whole in the moment. When we experience joyfulness, we are satisfied and pleased with things as they are. And last but not least, Joy deepens our relationship with individuals, with our work and with our community.

Has this ever happened to you?

Have you ever been to a networking event where you stumbled successfully upon an individual and before you can introduce yourself, they take the lead and start telling you everything you can imagine about them self?

Now picture this. They're doing all the talking, and you can't seem to get a word in edge wise. After approximately five minutes, they say "It was a pleasure meeting you," and then they leave to go find someone else to talk to. You meet them, you have no chance to tell them about yourself, they did all the talking, and then they tell you it was a pleasure meeting you and they leave.

Most people I speak with have the impression that they really didn't get anything from the exchange because they really have no understanding of *who you are.* But I want to challenge your thinking just a bit, and ask you to remove yourself from the equation to understand the real power of what just took place.

What might the person have gotten from the exchange? The answer is a joyful experience of them self. It's that simple. You provided a forum for them to feel good about them self. In my opinion, it doesn't get any better than that. If you can get out in the community and provide joyful experiences for others by listening to their story, their entire story, and their entire story first, then you'll find yourself on the path of heightened friendships and deepened relationships with others.

From a slightly different angle, here is one more example Jane experienced while attending an American Management Association (AMA) Conference in Boston several years ago.

Jane: While sitting on a bench at the end of a long day watching people move about the conference arena, a gentleman sat down beside me. He confessed that he hadn't registered for the conference, saw what was going on, and decided to check it out. Essentially he crashed the conference. I wondered what about the conference interested him. When I asked, I learned he was a consultant specializing in working with people in transition. The more we talked, the more interested I became in the kinds of retreats that he and his partner facilitated. In my own business in training and development, it was an approach to working with people I hadn't considered. As a result of the conversation, he invited me to attend an introduction and debriefing session a few blocks from the conference center that very evening. He indicated that he had other plans but that he would let his retreat partner know that I was coming. I was intrigued and decided to go. That evening I met a group of twenty people who were in all stages of transition. It was a powerful evening and although I was greatly enjoying the AMA conference, this event far exceeded the experiences that I was having. In just minutes, this gentleman matched my interest with his, and provided a joyful experience, one which continues to inspire me. He did this by inviting me to an event where I learned new methods of working with a multitude of individuals who are moving from one life stage to another, and ultimately helped me strengthen my awareness of the work that I could offer in my practice.

Thinking Points for Connecting Forward

- Are you noticing how your process contributes to creating exuberance and individual and collective joy?
- What changes can you make in how you show up that will contribute to the joy of others?
- What actions can you take today that will provide joy to at least one other person?

Summary

The essence of this strategy is that there are many ways to provide joyful experiences. One powerful way is to encourage the expression of someone's story. Listening and truly hearing another's story provides a joyful experience, bringing the best of each of you to the interaction. Bringing creativity and a fresh approach to all your interactions incorporates joy and escalates your relationships to the next level. Whew, how enlivening is that?

In Strategy Six, paying attention to the smallest of details makes the big difference.

> *The greatest gift of all is to provide a joyful experience to others.*
>
> **Ron Sukenick**

Chapter 11

Strategy Six

Consistently Doing The Little Things: *Make a Big Difference*

> *Life is made up of little things. True greatness consists in being great in little things.*
>
> **Charles Simmons**

Jane: At a conference a few years ago, an individual sitting at my table asked me, after hearing of my work in conflict resolution, if he could bend my ear. Responding to my nod, he went on to tell me that he and his law partner were severing their practice as a result of his partner violating a core principle and putting the practice at risk. He felt considerable anger and was having trouble keeping his emotions in check as he and his partner dissolved the partnership. I told him that I had a book that might be helpful, *Getting to Resolution* by Stewart Levine. The next day I dropped it off to him and I asked him if he could create a new vision of the relationship with his partner. He realized he had to let go of both the expectations he had previously held of their 15 year partnership and his current judgment of his partner's actions. He said, *"I guess what I really want is for both of us to learn from this, to appreciate how we've helped each other over the years, and to separate in a way that is emotionally and financially healthy for both of us."* I asked him if he thought he could keep that aim in mind as he moved forward, and he softly said he thought he could. A year later, he contacted me, thanked me, and said that both he and his partner had been on their own for some time now and were both doing well. It was a small act on my part that took no more than an hour, and made a big difference in his life and that of his partner.

Very early in my career, I realized that most people base their decisions about others on the experiences they have had with the person. At the foundation of positive experiences is a sense of trust. How do we develop a relationship of trust? Ron and I see it this way: a relationship of trust develops through *consistency*. In keeping the promises you make or letting the individual know when you are unable to. How basic is that?! In addition, there is another way we want to talk about consistency, and that is *consistently* doing the little things that *naturally* emerge as you learn about the needs and interests of another person. It is a dynamic and flowing process in which we give of ourselves, our resources, and our time. And it comes from our ability to pay attention!

Here is an example. You find out a person has accepted a new position where they will be selling to a brand new market. You have an article or a book that you believe would help them, such as my example above and send it to them: a helpful and straightforward process. Or perhaps, you know someone who is looking for the services or products the individual is marketing, and you put the individuals in touch with each other: the *matchmaking* of business relationships!

Making a Difference One Person at a Time

When I was still in corporate life, there was a time when I was quite overwhelmed by the time and attention needed by the hundreds of people with whom I worked. I was having a very difficult time in my desire to respond to the multitude of competing needs by the organization and by employees hungry for coaching, development, continuous improvement, support and resources. A good friend told me a story he thought would help me in my struggle, and this small act made a big difference to me. He told me about a man walking along a beach at one of the world's great oceans and seeing thousands of starfish, as far as he could see, washed up along the shore. He spotted one lone man as he got closer, throwing the starfish one by one back into the ocean. As he approached the man, he said *"what possible difference can you make. You'll never be able to throw all these starfish out into the sea. Why try?"* The man smiled compassionately while still throwing the starfish out, and replied gently, *"I just made a difference to that one."*

Ways to Make a Difference

There are countless examples of how we can make a difference in the lives of the individuals in our business and personal relationships: providing resources, connecting individuals with complementary needs, inviting individuals to networking meetings, sending out an article of interest. For Ron and me in the writing of this book, individuals read our chapters and gave us feedback and encouragement.

It's About Knowing People

Ron: What I've grown to realize and accept over the years is this one simple fact. The more we know about people, the more likely we can help. But the real question is this: What does it take to know people? How about this for an answer: What I've learned from years of interaction and observation, is that it takes approximately 2000 hours to get to know anyone. To put this into perspective, let me illustrate it this way. Working 40 hours a week for 50 weeks, would be 2000 hours. Now the question, how likely is it that you will be able to devote 2000 hours in any given year to getting to know someone? In my opinion it is not likely, but should this be a goal of ours? In my world, while the number of 2000 certainly reflects one's commitment to building the relationship, and I suggest that you start on this road, it's also important that each and every one of us take the time to pause, and to pace ourselves on how we build our relationships.

Increased Interaction Brings Increased Cooperation

How true it is when it comes to building solid relationships with others. Take a moment and think about rolling a pair of dice. If we asked you to roll one of the dice it would be called a die.

As you know, most die are numbered from 1 to 6 right? OK, now here's the question.

If you roll the die 20 times in a row, and the die lands on the number 3, what are the odds that the next time you roll the die it will land on the number 3? Now don't rush into it. Think for a moment.

Now most people that I mention this to say one of two things:

The odds are *not* very likely
OR
The odds are very likely

The reality is that in both cases the odds are the same. They are one in six.

With that said, what's most interesting about this formula, is the magic number of 6.

Now, let us contrast rolling dice to increasing interaction. Increasing interaction brings increased cooperation with others.

From my own observations, and from self research, my theory is that if you can interact with someone at least six times, then you'll end up having a 50/50 chance of either building an incredible relationship or not having a relationship at all.

While I'm open to having a relationship with others, it's only through mutual consideration that a relationship is possible. If you consider that the interaction you had could lead into an incredible relationship with someone then it is so. It's that simple.

So what is it I'm saying you ask? I'm saying that if you are interested in pursuing a relationship with another, make the attempt to interact at least six times from the time you first meet them.

By doing this, you're in a position to continue to lay the foundation toward building a wonderful relationship with another.

When all is said and done, just being there is never enough. Follow-up, increased interaction, and a sincere approach to the relationship is a winning combination.

Here's a Fun Net*Being* Exercise

As you're getting ready to leave the next networking event you attend, consider doing this. Make a concerted effort to make one last round for the sole purpose of saying goodbye to others, particularly saying goodbye to those whom you have met for the first time. You'll be amazed at how an additional 10-15 minutes of your time will affect others and how much your effort will be appreciated. It's a small but powerful way to develop relationships with new contacts. It is the little thing that makes a big difference.

How to Interact Six Times

Here's a simple method to the madness in building six interactions into your relationships.

1. You meet someone for the first time.
2. You send an e-mail stating that you enjoyed the interaction and look forward to seeing them again in the future.
3. If you have something in common, and you think that a project can be initiated or a partnership can be put in place, suggest that you get together.
4. Get together with the person.
5. After you've been together, thank them for taking the time to meet with you.
6. Stay in touch.

Jane: What is happening in the greater environment that impacts both of you, or the larger world? Let me give you an example. A few weeks after I met Ron, I attended a business roundtable group where Ron was kicking off the session. It was the day after September 11th. Ron beautifully brought the room of 80 people together by opening with, "Look around the room. Really look at each person at your table and at the surrounding tables. Look into their eyes, wave across the room, nod your head. Really see the person." What Ron did in that moment was to bring us cohesively together, to join us in our combined sadness around what was happening in our world. He didn't have to say out loud that which was still unspeakable. He was simply aware that we all had a common bond and he honored each of us by helping us simply see each other. A small action?

> You see, people that network call when they need something. People that are **Net***Being*, stay in touch.

Perhaps. But it certainly made a big difference that morning and it certainly made a big difference for me when considering whether to collaborate with him on this writing project.

Thinking Points for Connecting Forward

- The awareness of "the little thing" will come forward in interaction. Knowing what that is will come forward when you listen beyond the words.
- Introduce people to each other who you believe could help each other.
- Ask people, what "one thing" would help them right now move their personal or professional life forward. Help them by providing resources, or connecting them with others to make it possible.

Summary

This strategy has emphasized the power of small acts and how through consistently doing the little things, we make a big difference in the lives of countless others. Who knows, perhaps the world!

Now, move on to creating visibility, Strategy Seven, which focuses on multiplying efforts of exposing yourself to new and exciting possibilities and meeting and deepening relationships.

All that is meaningful grows from relationships; it is within this vortex that the future will be forged........"

Kenneth J. Gergen, Author and Professor of Psychology

Chapter 12

Strategy Seven

Creating Unparalleled Visibility: *Learning to Be Seen and Heard*

> *The real voyage of discovery consists not in seeking new landscapes but in having new eyes.*
>
> **Marcel Proust**

Ron: Achieving consistent visibility plays an important role in our ability to sustain successful relationships with others.

Moving to Indianapolis, Indiana in January 1988, not knowing anyone, my mission was simply to meet as many people as possible.

I have always liked meeting people and it's been easy for me being somewhat of an extrovert. I told a friend that I would set a goal to meet no less than about 10,000 people a year. I did just that.

Forming the Indiana Business Network, currently known as BNI (Business Network International), a must organization for all net workers, I then quickly moved into the mainstream of movers and shakers networking in the Indianapolis business community.

The visibility was great. Imagine the opportunity to meet and greet dozens of new people weekly in a controlled strong contact-networking environment where the sole purpose of our gathering was to build long lasting relationships and share business opportunities with one another. I'm sure that you would agree it was a great place to be.

Over the course of seven years, I met an average of 10,000 people a year. Averaging 28 people a day for seven years, there's no mystery to the benefits that followed.

If all the people I connected with knew between 200 to 300 people, then I would literally have access to between 2 to 3 million people. Wow! It would feel unbelievable to truly gain access to so many contacts.

But as you are learning, and as I have learned from this experience, it is not about how many people you meet or how many contacts you make. It is about the connection. How do you go about converting the contacts you make into connections that serve one another for a lifetime? Well, as I'm sure you sense, that's what the entire focus of this book is about.

Targeted Visibility: Intentional & Focused Approach

Targeting your visibility involves choosing those focus groups where your goals and objectives align to the objectives of others within these groups.

There are countless ways we meet people just by following interests. To meet people that align with your interests, you must pay attention to how you are spending your time, what you are saying yes to, and with whom. Your visibility will take on a life of its own, multiplying exponentially.

Create Visibility: The Stages to Play On

Networking groups: See the Appendix to view how you gain access to more than 250 viable and vibrant networking groups and associations nationally. Visit as a non-member and see if the association is for you.

Business cards and brochures: Hand out information about what you do including how they might contact you, so they better understand what you do. It's a natural and expected ritual, and it's economical. This information takes on a life of its own. You never know when an individual will come across this information and reconnect with you, or refer it to someone else.

Attending workshops, seminars, and conferences: There is never a substitute for facts information and knowledge. Get out and align yourself with others who share your goals and objectives.

Chamber of Commerce after hours and other chamber events: This is a great place to show up to meet lots of interesting people who will enjoy meeting you as well, and it is a casual contact networking opportunity. If you're not a member of your local chamber, we strongly suggest that you join one.

Create a Newsletter: A great way to deliver persistent presence is to send out a reoccurring message about what you do. An electronic newsletter is cost effective and does just that. Go to www.constantcontact.com to learn how easy it is.

Writing articles, books: Let people understand how you think and what you're thinking about. Writing about your passion is a clear road to both enhanced relationship and visibility success.

Embrace every opportunity to speak: You have to be seen, and you have to be heard. Every speaking opportunity supports the bottom line of all your NetBeing efforts.

Lead workshops, seminars, and conferences: What expert knowledge do you possess? Take the opportunity to develop and deliver this expertise in multiple settings demonstrating your knowledge and its application.

Hobbies and athletics: What is your hobby or exercise of choice? If you are preparing for the marathon, join a running or walking group. If you enjoy writing as a hobby or as a want-to-be author, join a writing group. There are endless groups that support hobbies and athletics, and lead to friendships and business relationships along the way.

Thinking Points for Connecting Forward

- Think about your current methods for connecting with others and establishing visibility.
- Think about recommendations made within this strategy to increase visibility. Which new methods will you consider?
- Think "outside the box." What method not recommended here would increase your visibility and reflect your unique relationship needs?

Chapter 12

Summary

Increasing visibility increases your ability to be seen and heard. Multiple ways to increase visibility have been presented. By focusing on meeting people who align with your interests, you accelerate the possibility for business and personal success.

Now connect the dots and move right into Strategy Eight, Make the Connection.

> *There is a larger field of possibilities; it is first our seeing what is out there and then following that which makes sense to us that will then lead to increasing meaningful visibility.*
>
> **Jane George-Surges**

Chapter 13 Strategy Eight Make the Connection: Connecting the Dots

> *The greatest gift I can conceive of having from anyone is to be seen by them, heard by them, to be understood and touched by them. The greatest gift I can give is to see, hear, understand and to touch another person. When this is done I feel contact has been made.*
>
> **Virginia Satir**

Jane: When I was a young child, my mother would often use contact paper as wall paper in one of her many household improvement projects. Sometimes as good as the contact paper was, it would still not adhere well or would bubble or crease up. The wall or the cabinet board that my mother was applying the paper to may not have been compatible. Perhaps there was moisture in the air, or other factors that contributed to non-cohesion, preventing good contact from taking place.

This is also true in relationship. You meet someone. You feel an attraction. You suspect good contact could take place between the two of you. Your intention may be to connect your experience to their experience. His intention may be to sell you something: a coaching session, a workshop, etcetera. While there's nothing negative about selling something or asking for a sale, the purpose of this strategy is to intend at a level beyond that. Becoming curious and asking questions beyond what you do for a living when it rises up in you to do so: making the kind of contact Virginia Satir speaks about in her quote.

Perhaps you find yourself not making good contact. I know I have. I may be excitedly talking about a workshop I'm presenting or a writing project, and later I've felt that I missed an opportunity to "meet" the other. Perhaps I missed the person in my pursuit of self-promotion, my interest in an external intention of making a living for example. While I want to stress that this is okay, the focus of this strategy is to connect from the inside out: a heart to heart contact.

The phrase "new intelligence" is sprinkled into the text to explore another way of looking at relationships. New intelligence in this context is enhanced thinking about what you already know! This strategy focuses on enhanced thinking about what you already know *intuitively* as it pertains to the role of making connections. This is taking the intuitive way with a new level of intention, understanding, and purpose.

The Power of Making the Connection

Ron: In the book *The Power of Flow*, Charlene Belitz and Meg Lundstrom share ideas on how you transform your life with meaningful coincidence. They talk about a day in which you make every green light and slip effortlessly into a parking spot in the most crowded part of town.

You make a to-call list, and the people on it call you first. You turn on the radio just in time to hear the exact information you need. As you think about a new career direction, you bump into a friend you haven't seen in years, who tells you of an exciting job opportunity.

These coincidences are called synchronicity, and according to Belitz and Lundstom are sure signs that you're in the flow; we say that you're in tune with making the connection.

Making the connection is hard to define. It's a *higher* force at work that seems to help align intention with outcome.

Regardless of how you describe the term, psychologist Mihaly Csikszentmihalyi says it well when he defines being in the flow as *"optimal experience, a state of concentration so focused that it amounts to absolute absorption in an activity."*

Jane: Synchronicity is the coming together of inner and outer events in a way that cannot be explained by cause and effect, and that is meaningful to the observer.

Synchronous events are possible each and every day.

The more aware we are of our self and our surroundings, the more likely it is that making the connection will occur. Ron and I believe that possessing certain internal characteristics will help strengthen the possibilities for these synchronistic connections to take place.

- **Commitment:** Your commitment to your own growth and expansion keeps you tuned in to what is constantly possible.
- **Mutuality:** You want for the other as you want for yourself. Mutual regard and mutual success permeates the exchange.
- **Courage:** You are willing to take the risk to reach out to others.
- **Focus:** You remember your aim as you move throughout your day.
- **Passion:** An intense, driving feeling moves through and with you.
- **Immediacy:** You have the quality or state of being "ready," of being able to respond in the moment.
- **Openness:** You are receptive to ideas and people's feelings.
- **Positivism:** You focus on the positive in ways you connect rather than individual differences that disconnect.
- **Giving to the World:** Promoting the best possible outcome for your partner separate from your self.

Connecting the Dots

Connecting the dots from a relationship "feeling" standpoint is intangible. It's the synchronicity described above, calling for focus, clarity, and direction, as we move toward mutual results.

The Law of Gravity states that every particle in the universe is attracted to every other particle! Gravity is what organizes things on the microscopic level. It's what holds things together: the solar system, the galaxy, the universe. What dynamic causes this to occur on a human level? Perhaps it is the same gravitational pulls, metabolic attraction and biological forces that operate on a universal level.

We are part of an interdependent and ever changing community. *I feel a connection* we've said from time to time when we've met someone personally or professionally who we would like to know further. This feeling takes us into the relationship and helps us move toward connection: a feeling energy that illuminates the path before us, causes excitement, and even feels mysterious or mystical. We cannot argue with it! *Who are you? Who am I? What is possible between us?* Now, you might be wondering if I am talking about a personal connection here. Yes, AND this *feeling* energy is present in business relationships as well.

Initiating Contact

Ron: Consider how many decisions you made since getting up this morning. Did you decide to initiate a conversation with someone new? Did you decide to call someone you've recently met and follow up on a conversation? How do you go about taking the first step, the second step, the third step, and so on? It is with risk and trepidation that we often decide to initiate contact. More importantly, it is with *intention* and *attention* that can really make the difference. What is my intention as I consider another person? Is my intention to really see them and be seen by them? How do I attend to this process in what we call business or professional relationships?

Intention & Attention

Jane: Today business and professional relationships are typically formed around projects. In fact, futurists say we are heading toward the age of no careers, where we come together around a series of projects. These projects will likely be compensated in a multitude of ways. In the relationships that form traditionally, the project comes first. We then look for someone who has the qualifications, experience, financial backing, or connections that make sense for this particular project. The primary considerations for the relationship to exist are often driven by our intellect, logic, and facts.

This other energy offers yet another dimension in our coming together. We respond to a feeling attraction, this sense that we are to do something together, and the project *emerges from the relationship.*

Let us back track for a moment as it pertains to going into relationship with *intention* and *attention.* Intention is the direction toward a specific destination that I have chosen for my life. Intention is purposeful and comes from the purpose of my life. Attention is watching and awareness *along the way.*

Let us suppose a feeling attraction exists between you and me, and that we sense that there is something we are to do together. The intention is the possibility of creation between us. The attention I experience is to stay with the possibility and pay attention to what emerges along the way.

Interested in providing tools for transformation, Tom Lane, *The Way of Quality*, says for him it's like going hiking. Where he is going is the intention, and watching each step along the way is attention. Attuning to what happens along the path and what sensations emerge guide the way.

Awareness, Excitement, Energy, Choice, & Initiate

Continuing to connect the dots from the "I" to the "we," individually and collectively, we become more aware of what we are drawn to, respond to the excitement that builds, and follow the energy of choice to initiate and move toward collaboration and partnership.

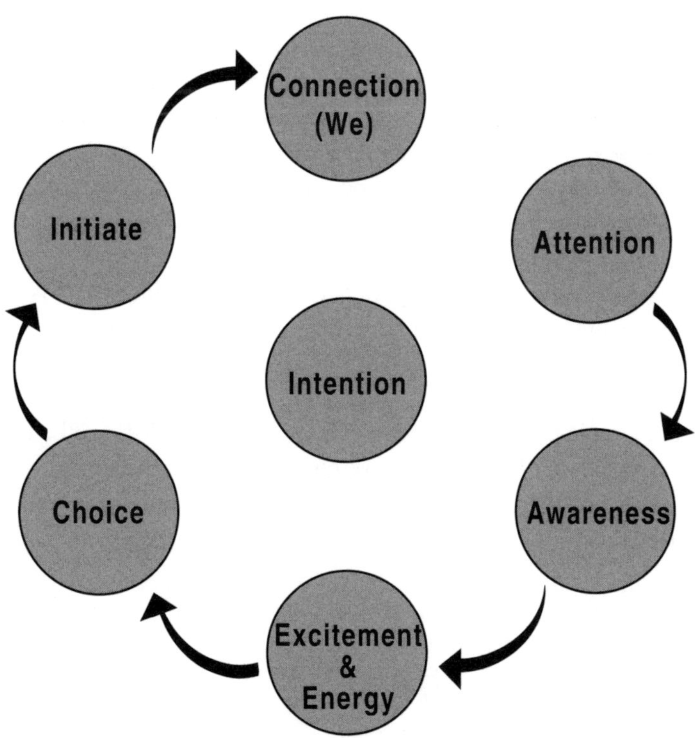

From our *intention*, we *attentively* and watchfully attend to that which comes along. We pay attention to our environment, that which draws us, and we also pay attention to messages from our bodies, such as our eyes meeting another. We become aware of an attraction and desire to know this person. We feel excitement and energy build, and then go to a choice point. We choose our next response, and initiate contact. From there, the connection is made with the person if the person is open. At any point, we can take ourselves out of making this connection. With attention all the way through this process and with practice, we are aware of our thought process that prevented us from following through. Perhaps we are not sure if there is a reciprocal attraction (especially in the boy-girl dance), or perhaps if we are initiating a business contact and the person is a well known professional with individuals lining up to meet him or her, we may be hesitant. There are many reasons we do not continue ahead toward making the connection; attention to our process will help provide information noticing where we block ourselves, and continue to strengthen our ability to become more contactful, and improve our connection skills. A bit of caution here. Sometimes not following through to connection is also the best choice.

Becoming Contactful

Virginia Satir's quote at the beginning of this chapter helps us speak to this. We'll repeat it again: *The greatest gift I can conceive of having from anyone is to be seen by them, heard by them, to be understood and touched by them. The greatest gift I can give is to see, hear, understand, and to touch another person. When this is done I feel contact has been made.*

What is wonderful about the experience of being in this world is we have opportunities time and time again to show up again, to experiment again at coming from a quieter, more present place.

Initiating a connection doesn't guarantee that a connection will be made. As you experiment with becoming more contactful (improving your ability to make good contact), you will simply improve your chances for a good connection to occur.

We are different with every person we meet. In fact we are different with the same person each time we meet, because we are never the same person. Being in the flow with others help us "faith it" that there are possibilities for connection.

Think of a time when you felt the flow for you. Take a moment to write or reflect on that experience. I'll hold your space for you.

Welcome back.

Timing: From Intention to Connection

Connecting the dots from initial feeling attraction to actual collaboration may take a moment, five minutes or a lifetime. It is truly a journey: a journey that may only become clear when you look back; a journey which began synchronistically.

Is synchronism something we can control or influence? If so, how? What can we do to enhance or influence synchronicity? Pause for a moment to consider the offering below of thinking points to help you increase synchronicity in your life and to move toward connection.

Thinking Points for Connecting Forward

- Suspend a direct route to a "project."
- Clarify your own intention.
- Look for mutuality.
- Slow down by using breathing or other techniques that help you quiet your mind.
- Become aware of energy and excitement through attention to feelings and physiological responses.
- Notice yourself and your surroundings. Synchronicity may be difficult to recognize.
- Experiment with taking risks in initiating contact.
- Experience your experience of the experience!
- Remember that being contactful is not predicated on making the connection.
- Experiment and practice, practice, practice.

A few do's and don'ts: Don't overanalyze or be self critical. Do play with experiment. Don't take the experience too seriously. Do remember if the person walks away from you, your intention is to be in the world in a contactful and caring way. They are simply where they are. It's a lifetime of experiment.

Summary

You may argue against this and feel that *it is too nebulous. You can't get your arms around it. It's too touchy-feely.* Calling for a *suspension of disbelief*, imagine for a moment a time when you were led by your feelings. You put caution to the wind and your logical planning aside and with a leap of faith made a decision to follow something, some idea, some person, some job, some cause. What happened? Or, perhaps you put logic first and didn't follow. Any regrets? In conversation with others, the answer many give is no regrets even when they didn't like the outcome and connections weren't made, and regrets when not following. You decide. Enjoy the process. Enjoy the journey.

Now, on your mark, speedily go to Strategy Nine, Travel at the Velocity of a fast-paced World.

> *It is so beautiful this looking for the beautiful…its so connecting this looking for the connecting.*
>
> **Jane George-Surges**

Chapter 14

Strategy Nine
Travel at the Velocity of a Fast-Paced World: *Flowing at the Speed of Change*

Great men accomplish significant deeds through an enduring effort in a consistent direction. When you wish to achieve an important aim, direct your thoughts along a steady, uninterrupted course.

Proverb 57, I Ching

Jane: Several months ago, I had an air duct company provide a quote on cleaning my chimney, ducts and vents throughout my house. Two individuals from this reputable company came to my house. They were very professional and personable, and I felt very comfortable in going forward. However, with other more immediate needs I was facing with the purchase of this 75 year old house and more than a bit of chaos in my process, I put the work on hold. Now, I'm ready to do the work but can't remember the name of the company and can't find the quote. I initially found their name in the yellow pages but none of the names now look familiar. Here is my point. This company did a great job getting in and providing a quote. They were friendly and knowledgeable representatives of the company. What they didn't do is keep their name in front of me by providing a follow up letter or call. I didn't have a good system in place that kept their name in front of me either. The relationship was made but it wasn't sustained by either one of us. There is urgency for me now to have this work done, and their contact information is lost. My loss and theirs!

This often happens in relationship. It is living in this fast-paced world with the ability to see the forest and the trees that is critical. In doing so, we cultivate our ability to see what is needed, to make decisions, and to respond to the flow of personal and professional relationships all around us. We flow with the constantly changing variables, and don't lose each other along the way!

Three Phases of Approaching Change

Order & Stability
(Clarity & Precision)
Current State
Awareness

Planning & Preparation
(Alignment)
Unknown

Possibility & Imagination
(Choices)
Readiness

Responsiveness is a powerful contribution we can make to living in a hurried society. Some may call this responsiveness a competitive advantage, and, yes, while it is or certainly can be, we also offer another view. New openings and new possibilities emerge constantly. Relationships are critical to making things happen. We are the competitive advantage as we respond and move with the velocity of the fast-paced world all around us. The strategy we offer here, then, is to add speed to the discussion of building relationships cautioned by alignment.

Building relationships quickly builds greater confidence and strengthens the possibility of synergy between people. By building the relationship NOW, you become a resource to others quickly, saving their time down the road when a need arises.

Flowing at The Speed of Change

Ron: Evan Walters, our friend and independent editor, suggested how riding in an automobile down the highway illustrates this point. Look out the window while traveling at a speed of 65 MPH. The grass at the roadside passes in a blur, but every detail of the car next to you also moving at 65 MPH is easily comprehended. But if you stand by the highway as the cars pass, they seem to pass in a blur.

We live in a fast-paced world. Everything is moving so rapidly that it passes us in a blur, or we pass it without noticing, or we are simply out of step with the rest of the world. Sometimes that is a good thing! The ability to focus on details or to understand the big picture is dependent on several factors. 1.) The velocity of our own movement. 2.) Our ability to slow down in the midst of chaos. 3.) The ability to look from many directions at the same situation: sometimes traveling at the same speed such as in our 65 miles an hour metaphor, and sometimes standing by the side of the road quietly observing.

Take a moment and answer the following questions.

1 What significant changes can I make to become more responsive to the needs of others?

2 How do I respond to the increased urgency of others while keeping my own aims in sight?

3 Do I listen to the needs and ideas of others to improve my efficiencies and effectiveness?

4 How does my own sense of clarity help me in making decisions to quickly and effectively respond to another?

5 What concerns do I have? What influence do I have concerning those issues?

Rudyard Istvan, a former Vice President with the Boston Consulting Group, is a leading proponent of what is often called "time based strategy." He believes that in the future, speed, even more than cost or quality, will be a big player in success. We invented fast food, one-hour dry cleaning, instant coffee, drive through banking, on-line commerce, and accelerated learning. Need we say any more?

While we see quality as an essential thread, we concur with Mr. Istvan and add that strong relationships that you have either developed or are in the process of developing will outweigh everything else. In essence, people will base their buying or partnering decisions on the relationships they have in place and are actively growing.

It seems that most people literally develop a wait and see attitude. *We just met. Who knows where the relationship will go. Relationships take time.*

Does that sound like you? Relationships do take time. But why not move quickly into the possibility of building a wonderful, long lasting relationship? Building urgency into our relationships creates a proactive approach to enhancing the results we desire.

When we act on the possibility of building relationships with others, when we are proactive, we become the prime moving force or "relationship builder." Our chance for a stronger and more productive relationship is heightened. Being proactive as we face change creates excitement and enthusiasm. And with excitement and enthusiasm comes the potential for greater success and opportunities with others.

Thinking Points for Connecting Forward

- In the fast-paced world that you are a part of, do you have a touchstone to help you "stay the course" as you respond to the needs of others on a project?
- As you flow at the speed of change, are you vigilant to maintaining alignment between what you are doing and the intentions you have for your life?
- Are you taking initiative with new or old relationships when you see a natural fit between your objectives and theirs?
- Are you distinguishing between responsiveness and reaction, and attuning your actions accordingly?
- Is the velocity of the fast-paced world taking you where you want to go?

Summary

Speed is a driving force. When we're meeting individuals, we are meeting them one at a time and the opportunity to quickly move into a relationship posture is now! Focusing time and attention then is a quickening fueled by possibility, alignment, precision, and clarity as we move forward at the speed of change.

Let's now focus on shortening learning curves in Strategy Ten, the essence of which is moving yourself and your partner toward *fulfilling your dreams.*

> *Fueled by precision and clarity, embrace the possibilities that are a product of the velocity and change all around you.*
>
> **Jane George-Surges**

Chapter 15

Strategy Ten
Shorten Learning Curves: *Move Into Dream Fulfillment*

> *A glorious thing when one has not unlearned what it means to begin.*
>
> **Martin Buber**

Jane: This strategy is about shortening learning curves to move you toward fulfilling your and your relationship partner's dreams. It invites you to walk purposively in the world, embracing each person you meet with new eyes. Your task is to determine what it is you are to do together, and how your relationship might support both of you. Perhaps you are to simply share a smile, and the relationship is complete; perhaps there is a project you are to do together that will reveal itself over time, projecting both of you toward realizing your dreams.

Walking purposively and looking at each person in this way, is the first step toward shortening a long process of discovering what this *doing* might be. Shortly after I moved to Indiana, I accepted a position with a gentleman who had visions to grow his organization all over the state and throughout the United States. He had four different sites at the time. When we met, the first thing he said to me was, *"what is it we are to do together?"* What I found is that was all! That question was his gift to me. He presented and I received a question that would be with me at the forefront of meeting other people along the way…what is it we are to do together?

This strategy also emphasizes the momentum that develops when you find common ground quickly. The following provides yet another way to approach shortening learning curves.

Chapter 15

Common Ground Where the Project Arises

Finding common ground will help you jointly move toward dream fulfillment.

The project we are to do together is revealed when we find our overlapping purpose and intention. Common ground. Let's talk about the word *project.* We are using it here in two different ways.

To **pro**-ject refers to a future state: looking ahead. We are **pro-**jecting into the future a potential outcome. When we see we have choices, we come up with projects to achieve this projection! The project is an undertaking, tangible plan or design that casts us forward. **Pro**-ject: forward looking. Pro-**ject:** forward doing.

Out of the contact that takes place between you and the person you are meeting comes the project. Again, it may be a small project and the project is quickly concluded. Or it may be a large project involving many hours, months, or years and great rewards. Stating this again, the project emerges out of the relationship.

Building Context

What is context and how do we use it to project us forward? The power is in your ability to put into context the information you are constantly receiving in the meeting with another.

Context considers the environment, situation, relationship, and language that supports the connection we are trying to make. For example, when I teach a leadership course, I occasionally throw in words like concentric circles and quantum physics. If I don't tie these words into the discussion, they appear totally out of context or out in left field, and I begin to lose people. People ask if they are in the wrong room. The language and the appropriateness of the conversation in a given setting helps us to set up and establish common context.

The environment also is an important consideration. Individuals have told me about going to lunch with a customer and being told that their customer-supplier relationship was ending due to poor performance or inadequate quality. The interruptions of the restaurant server, the laughter of other patrons, the clanking of dishes, and the brightness of the room contrasted to the information being conveyed. The restaurant environment didn't fit the message.

Building context, then, is the art of paying attention to environment, the situation at hand, the language used, and weaving together information derived from communication, insight, observations, impressions, and intuition. This is the task of both individuals in the relationship as they strive to make a connection and shorten learning curves.

There are compelling reasons to build context into shortening learning curves.

Building context helps us use our time more efficiently and effectively. Time is a premium for most of us. A context orientation helps us direct our communication to what is most important and align our doing accordingly.

For example, if I am on my way out the door for a trip to Chicago and Ron calls to talk about a section of the book, how I respond helps set the tone. I tell him that I'm running late and about to get in my car and drive north.

Attending to where I am, Ron may alert me to construction problems along the route or a pending storm that may affect me. For example, he may say *hey, I just made that trip recently, and you'll want to watch out for construction right around the I80-94 tollway. You may want to consider an alternate route.* In that moment Ron has gone to what is most important to me: the context that I am in currently.

From there, he might go to our joint context, and ask if I have time to listen to a few ideas he has about the book. If I am contextually aware of the decisions that we are currently making, and we are about to go to press for example, what he has to say becomes figural. I realize that he and I need to make a decision now so that he, or we, can progress forward.

Depending on the urgency, the schedule, and other factors, we determine together how and when to proceed in communication.

Chapter 15

Context Awareness

Context awareness increases the ability to quickly determine that which is most important to the moment. Constantly checking in or attuning to the person as we discussed in the listening strategy, the communication proceeds accordingly. This builds the momentum and shortens learning curves, moving the project to dream fulfillment.

The Bad Dance

Individuals see a problem or issue from their own contextual viewpoint. Be aware of this propensity and how mechanical behavior can result. *When I act this way, you react that way, so I react this way, and you react that way.* Tom Lane refers to this as the bad dance. Learn to watch your process, your reactions and stop the dance if it is trending negatively.

Dream Fulfillment

Let me offer another example. Writing and publishing this book is currently the common ground and mutual context that Ron and I share. At some point, this project will be complete, and our paths may diverge. Remember the process of relation*shift.*

Project conclusions give way to new projects as we look ahead at other creative possibilities. Considering the multitude of choices we have separately and as partners, we will individually decide if and how these new projects align with what is most important to us.

If one of us proceeds in one direction, the other will find partners for his/her dream. As our relationship shifts, we may become helpful helpers to each other, not active partners. Communicating our dreams and aspirations as we go along and getting clear about the direction we would individually like to go, moves us more quickly into dream fulfillment in the next phase along our individual journey. Most importantly, we want for each other to find success and happiness in going forward.
Consider the following thinking points as you jointly look at how your experiences and dreams are matching up as you attend to your joint project.

Thinking Points for Connecting Forward

- Operate out of choice, not out of habit, as you work with the unique individual you are currently partnering with.
- Continuously realign frequency and quality of interaction as you move toward your desired outcome.
- Are the context and purpose of the relationship constantly being considered?
- Question your relationship process. Where is your partner right now? Where are you? Where are the two of you? Are you working on what needs to be worked on? Is there something else you need to be considering, to be doing?
- What improvements would help your process?
- Has the context of your relationship changed?
- Are you allowing your relationship to shift accordingly?

Identifying questions for self and the relationship, and continuously reviewing personal and relationship effectiveness will help you along the path toward dream fulfillment now and in the future.

Summary

This strategy encourages walking purposively in relationship with others and asking the question *what are we to do together.* While this question doesn't need to be asked aloud, keeping the question at the forefront of each meeting helps you pay attention to what is possible between you and another. Shortening your learning curve as your project together emerges, and as you move toward project completion calls for attention to context: the environment, the situation at hand, the language used, information, and the decisions important to moving forward. Continuously asking "process questions" such as how are you doing collaboratively, what needs to be done, how satisfied is your business partner, and how satisfied are you keeps you addressing process and project improvements along the way, shortening the learning curve as you go along.

Next, we're getting down to basics and introducing the strategy of bringing the ordinary to the extraordinary, giving muscle to the tried and true statement of far exceeding expectations.

> *When there is so much information coming toward us, remembering our purpose and finding context will help us move forward in relationship, in life, in love.*
>
> **Jane George-Surges**

Chapter 16

Strategy Eleven
Moving into Legendary Status: *Going from the Ordinary to the Extraordinary*

> *Our background and our environment influence how we respond in our dance in the world; what makes us extraordinary is when we choose to begin each day new and begin again and again and again responsible for who we are today and who we are becoming.*
>
> **Jane George-Surges**

Ron: I had the chance a few years back to host a radio talk show. It was a weekly Saturday morning get together of people who would interact with the audience sharing ideas, information and other resources.

The topics focused on building business strategies to use to create the level of success for which we are looking.

About a year and a half into the show, I realized that the demands were getting greater and that people's expectations were becoming unfulfilled.

So I did an informal survey asking the audience to call in, send in, or just tell me, *"What have you been doing to exceed people's expectation?"* The results were amazing.

After interacting with approximately 3,400 people, less than two percent could easily tell me what they do to exceed people's expectations.

In fact, 68% of the people felt that what they were currently doing was exceeding expectations because they would receive compliments for the work performed.

Unfortunately, it doesn't work that way.

Doing what is expected, doing a good job, or getting complements doesn't necessarily mean that you're exceeding people's expectations. It simply means that you're doing your job.

Ask yourself the following questions:

1. If you do a good job for someone, will they always do business with you?

2. If you do a good job for someone, will they always tell others about you?

The answer to the above questions is a resounding ***no!*** Unless you're exceeding people's expectations in the relationships you're developing, it is always possible for them to go elsewhere.

Here is an example from a Construction Project Manager. Let's call him Phil. Phil is well liked and knows his job well. Whenever he has a construction project to estimate, no one seems to do a better job. He always builds the project for less then the budget allows.

Now ask yourself another question: Is Phil exceeding people's expectations, or is he simply doing a great job? Or, from a cynical perspective, is it possible that Phil always over-budgets and just brings the project in for what it really took the company to build it?

Kind of gets you thinking, doesn't it?

You see, even though Phil might think that he is exceeding his company's expectations, he isn't. He is just doing a great job and the company knows it.

In fact because Phil always comes in below budget, the company expects that Phil will do just that: come in below budget.

So what can we learn from this story? Consider what Jane says in bold below

Going beyond the ordinary begins with looking for ways to help individuals in unexpected and surprising ways. Deepen your awareness of how you can naturally go beyond the every-day; doing the extraordinary begins and ends with evaluation and continuous improvement.

This is what I mean. As individuals, we can't just sit back and expect that what we have been doing is enough. We need to find out what we can do to really make a difference.

Some with whom we relate will know what they want and need. These people will articulate their expectations when we ask the appropriate questions.

Most people, however, will not know how to answer the question "what can I do to far exceed your expectations?" As Jane and I talked about this strategy, she said that it really gets down to paying attention and deeply questioning what *multiple* needs are building: raising your level of awareness and theirs of what is possible beyond the ordinary.

We dig the well before the thirst!

Here's an incredible story

Jim Cathcart, the author of the book *Relationship Selling,* tells a story that clearly illustrates how an individual went far beyond the standard operating procedure to far exceed one person's expectations.

Jim, a successful author, speaker and business consultant talks about his frequent visits to a local McDonald's where he has what he calls *Quiet Time.* Jim enjoys a time each morning where he gathers his thoughts, and plans for the day ahead.

Every time he goes there, he orders an egg McMuffin and a cup of coffee. One day, upon his arrival, he noticed two big buses parked in the parking lot. What do you think goes through his mind? You're right, he starts thinking that he will probably not have any quiet time this morning, and that he will have a long wait for breakfast.

He walks into the McDonald's and quickly goes to the end of the line. To his surprise, a woman comes from behind the counter to the back of the line and says, "Mr. Cathcart, your breakfast is ready."

Taking him by surprise, she walks him up to the front counter, and hands him his usual breakfast. Just as he prepares to pull out his wallet to pay for his purchase, she says, "Mr. Carthcart, breakfast is on me today."

Wow! Can you imagine something like that happening to you? Undoubtedly, Jim was blown away by this act of service.

Jim was absolutely surprised and delighted by this act, and went away from the experience thinking this is a special employee and a special McDonald's.

Does McDonald's teach their employees to provide these random acts of greatness, or did the employee simply do this on her own? In any case, it works. And from a relationship building standpoint, interactions like these will never go unnoticed.

A Look at Moving From Ordinary to Extraordinary: *A Process & Project Management Approach*

Jane: An extraordinary outcome will have at its foundation a process for managing the project that emerges between two people. As Ron recalls Jim Carthcart's McDonald's experience, many project management dynamics are at play in the exceptional service he received. Let me list them for you:

1. Jim identified, as part of his morning ritual, the same McDonald's, the same breakfast, and probably a favorite table.

2. The employee at McDonald's did something key here: she noticed!

3. An assumption I will make here is that she not only noticed that Jim ordered the same breakfast every visit; she also noticed that he was there for "quiet time."

4 She did not have to have a *chit-chat* relationship with him to know that his preference was to get his breakfast as fast and efficiently as possible, and find a quiet table to do his planning for the day. She paid attention to non-verbal cues through her observation skills.

5 She recognizes him, and quickly does the exceptional--she orders his breakfast, takes it to him, and pays for it!

6 She demonstrates attuning to his needs not only for breakfast but for quiet planning time. While she may not have been able to provide the quiet on that particular morning, she was able to provide the breakfast he wanted because she knew his preferences, and was able to provide it quickly. She took a process approach; she determined the process that was needed to provide customer service in this moment. She deviated from the standard operating procedures of a customer waiting in line, took immediate action, and responded accordingly, quickly, decisively and exceptionally.

Let's take this to another level then: the level of project management. A project emerges in relationship: a project to write a book, to partner in a customer-supplier relationship, or to partner on a business endeavor. Project management considers multiple factors to support successful completion. Relationships, resources, materials, support structures, and timeframes.

A process and project management focus will take you from the ordinary to the extraordinary, truly taking you to legendary status.

Thinking Points for Connecting Forward

- Shared visioning and purpose: what do we both want to see to ensure extraordinary satisfaction on both our parts?
- Identify planning, goal setting, and time tables to reinforce a shared focus.
- Establish ground rules to support the project. Who will do what? How will information be managed? What benchmarking might help identify best practices and learning from others?
- Establish process checks established along the way. Ask each other, "How can I help you?" Ask for help, "This is something I need your help with. Can you help me with this?" Gauge personal and shared satisfaction and make adjustments as needed. Don't let grievances build up. Identify your own resistances to bringing up conflict. Take personal responsibility for those resistances. Move through and let go of one-time events that cause frustrations. Address them if you aren't able to let go of them in a way that is respectful and moves you forward toward improving the relationship.
- Together identify needed resources, budgets, and support from others outside of your partnership.
- Collect information that will help support your project.
- At major completion points, review where you are, what is needed to go forward, and quality improvements that will help ensure the excellence you are both seeking.
- Think about where you believe you are doing a good job in providing a product, service or friendship for someone.
- Now take a moment to think about whether you are doing a good or a great job.
- What examples illustrate "good" or "great" for you?

Summary

A consistent focus in moving from the ordinary to the extraordinary moves us to legendary status. Rethinking what we do, looking for ways to become more resourceful, and having a process and project management focus will help establish this exceptional foundation.

We are now onto Strategy Twelve, Becoming Technologically Savvy: Building the Techno Advantage. As you better understand the vast technology and the multitude of communication infrastructures, you will be better able to choose the preferred communication medium for the relationship in front of you--helping you move information and retain and respond to the multiple relationships you have and will be forming.

> *Go beyond the ordinary and create the extraordinary.*
>
> **Ron Sukenick**

Chapter 17

Strategy Twelve
Become Technologically Savvy: *Building the Techno Advantage*

The best way to have a relationship is to make it convenient to have one.
Ron Sukenick

Jane: The on-going explosion of new technology shapes our ability to react and respond to the needs of others. It also shapes the future in building relationships. We are more and more technologically interdependent with our families, our friends, our communities, and our business partnerships. Think about the ease and speed of communication that takes place through the internet. How were any of us able to build or maintain relationships in the past? From on-line learning, to on-line family reunions, to on-line networking groups, to working on a project, to e-lawyering, we are able to electronically "meet" in the magical place of virtual reality. We are able to make connections literally all over the world twenty-four hours a day. The Internet has radically changed the way communication takes place. Considering the ease of being in business during this age of technology, we can thank our lucky stars for the multitude of communication forums that are available. How many of us could say that our business would exist today if it weren't for keeping up with technological innovations?

Why state the obvious so insistently? Most everyone already knows this, right? So what are we talking about here? In a world that has become so highly interactive, how we develop business partnerships and conduct business must take into consideration communication technology. There is a lot of discussion about the technology that is available today. In fact, in his article, *Future Watch: An Overview of Trends*, Lowell Wolff says that the rapidity of technological change will continue to accelerate. Get this. Wolff says that the next three decades will bring two centuries worth of change! Two centuries! In other words, he says, that in the next seven minutes, the same amount of change will occur as did in the last thirty years! Even non-tech people find this pretty exciting. It is also exciting to think of the potential of possibilities that arise from this phenomenon. As our possibilities increase, so does our need to increase our capability to better decide which technology will help support our business and our relationships. Being aware of the vast channels of communication and deciphering which of these channels to use in a given relationship and situation is also an important consideration.

This strategy reviews the major communication technologies present today, and provides thinking points for you to consider as you choose the communication channel that works for you and your business partner.

Developing a presence, technologically speaking, calls for examining the communication channels. To be out there in the business world, we must do our technological work.

A Technological Presence

While voice mail and fax communication will continue to exist and be expected, consider the following.

- Web Presence
- E-Commerce
- Internet Services
- Virtual Offices
- Teleconferencing
- Digital Communication
- Expert Systems

Web Sites

In his book *Net Future*, Chuck Martin states that for most customers, what they see at a company's web site determines their view of the company. A company is expected to have a web presence. While some companies allocate limited marketing dollars to maintain a minimal web presence, others are forging new relationships with their customers and redefining themselves for the on-line world.

The web provides unprecedented opportunity for companies to interact with organizations and individuals all over the world. What a contrast to what was done in the past! Now, in addition to company brochures and annual reports as the major forum for promoting organizations, with a web presence, you are literally only a fingertip away.

E-Commerce

The World Wide Web, a virtual commercial district, is here to stay. Customers book air travel, conduct home-line shopping, and surf the net to conduct business around the globe. This has allowed organizations to drastically cut their investments in inventories, lower the cost of real estate, and create new opportunities every single day. Warren Bennis talks about the future of banks reducing support to a computer, a person, and a dog. The person feeds the dog, and the dog is there to guard the computer. Fargo IBM is an example of this. Fargo IBM went from three floors of a downtown bank to three rooms according to Lowell Wolff in his *Future Watch* writings. With the ability to interact and the connectivity of interdependent technologies, this is just one example of technology's revolutionary impact on an organization.

The Internet

If you had to choose just one characteristic of the Internet that set it apart from just about everything else, surely it would be its interactivity. Quickly, efficiently, and effectively you are able to interact with others around the world.

A few weeks ago, I was on-line emailing a colleague of mine. An instant message appeared before me from an individual from London whom I had met flying from Detroit to Paris a few years ago. He was in Sweden working with a client. I chatted for a few minutes with him, and then noticed I had two pieces of mail in my in-box. I moved over to my mailbox, and pulled up an email from a friend and business partner from New Zealand. The other message was from family in France. In just minutes, time and distance were truly an illusion. Our world is getting smaller based on the many communication and technological vehicles that are available.

Chapter 17

Virtual Offices

We forecast that this trend will continue to grow exponentially. Information technologies make it possible to connect, to collaborate and to communicate easily from virtually anywhere: from your tractor if you are a farmer, from the restaurant down the street, from the airport, the car, and certainly from home. Voice mail, cell phones, teleconferencing, digital communication, and email make it possible to conduct business from wherever you are; making it even more possible *to be here now* as Ram Dass so wisely encouraged us to do several decades ago.

Just-in-Time Intelligence: *Expert Systems*

The very essence of a web search is that you can click on text or pictures and be transported instantly, or pretty quickly anyway, to somewhere else.

In addition, you can obtain expert knowledge in moments. Receiving information we need as we need it has become more readily available through computer-based applications that use a representation of human expertise in a specialized field of knowledge. According to the textbook *Organizational Behavior: Foundations, Realities, and Challenges 2003*, by Debra L. Nelson and James Campbell Quick, expert systems provide advice to non-experts, provide assistance to deepen your expertise, and serve as a training and development tool in organizations. Expert systems are used in medical decision making, diagnosis, and medical informatics. Anheuser-Busch uses an expert system to assist managers in ensuring that personnel decisions comply with antidiscrimination laws. Expert systems are on the rise as technology more and more meets up with the reality of our every day. To test this, go to your search engine now and key in expert systems. Enjoy your find. What a great tool to possess and to provide to others as they deepen their just-in-time-knowledge.

Technology will increase your business opportunities, and we're assuming that's what you want. Technology will help you better meet the expectations for responsive-paced communication, information gathering, improved customer service, greater efficiency, and ultimately to improve your capacity and ability to get things done.

The good news is that if you are just getting started, or need to bring your technology to the next level, resources are literally all around you. Talk to people in your business network and within your educational systems. You will receive information about affordability and you will also find that people will want to share their skills with you. See Part Three for more information to guide you in your technological growth.

Diagnosing Communication Channels

We've spent some time on major communication technologies available today. Just remember that every seven minutes, three decades worth of new technology is born. Now let's talk about how you choose to communicate with all the technology available. This section of the strategy emphasizes shifting from your own preferred style of communication when necessary to match your relationship partner when necessary.

The world has changed forever and as we deal with individuals one to one, we must consider negotiating and balancing between various paths of communication channels. Examples of various channels include from the still always effective one-on-one facc contact, or telephone, to more recent advances in communication such as e-mail, electronic bulletin boards, chat rooms, and virtual meetings.

As you look at these communication channels, which mode do you most prefer? Does it change as you think about a specific relationship? Does it change based on the discussion you wish to have? Of course it does. Now, have you thought about asking your partner about his or her preferred mode? It is important to remember that each one of us has a preferred channel of communication. The willingness to shift as we need to while keeping the situation and the relationship in mind will improve the ability to "meet" in the real and the electronic world.

Thinking Points for Connecting Forward

- Are you aware of the vast communication technology available?
- Have you identified your preferred communication channels?
- Have you asked your relationship partner their preferred communication channel, and discussed what modes will serve both of you?
- Are you constantly identifying the technological changes that will enhance your relationships and strengthen your business and professional life?
- What "Just-in-Time" Intelligence and expert systems would accelerate information learning?
- How are you attending to and maximizing your potential through technology?

Summary

Thanks to the Internet, and the latest innovations in technology, the confines of time and space have disappeared. Communication technology will help you better meet the increased expectations for the ever changing market. Strengthen your personal and business relationships by diagnosing the best channel for the specific relationship. Part Three provides additional resources for increasing your technological savvy. We are lucky to live in this time!

Next, we are onto *One World, One Playing Field*, a look at Strategy Thirteen, *Becoming a Global Partner.*

> *To be out there in the business world, we must do our technological work.*
>
> **Jane George-Surges**

Chapter 18

Strategy Thirteen

Becoming a Global Partner: *One World, One Playing Field*

> *...and I say to myself, what a wonderful world.*
>
> **Louis Armstrong**

Ron: We have all heard the expression "It's a small world, isn't it?" Typically two people are having a discussion when they begin to put multiple thoughts and connections together. From both present and past experiences they begin to say *"that's funny, do you know so and so? I know so and so. It's such a small world we live in, isn't it?"*

Well the fact is that it really isn't as small a world as we sometimes think. Actually as I tell people, it is a rather large world that we live in. Think about it. If you were to put this book down, jump into your car (by the way, be sure to take this book with you) and start driving in the furthest direction you can in the country you are in, you'll notice how large the world is.

At the same time, we know we live in an increasingly global marketplace. This strategy emphasizes that businesses of all sizes are treating the world as one playing field as individuals search the entire world for customers, suppliers, partnerships, and employees. The power, if you will, is knowing what to with the multitude of information, opportunities, and relationships that come your way, and taking into account the multiple factors important when doing business with individuals from another country. This is also true in the international communities in which we reside.

Jane: If you are reading this book sequentially, you've read Strategy 8, Make the Connection in Chapter 13. Strategy 8 relies heavily on trusting a feeling energy that moves you forward, where the project or working relationship comes second. In contrast to this feeling energy, Strategy 13 focuses on making decisions that intellectually guide you into the global marketplace. These are amazing times. Yet, this is also a time to wisely consider many factors.

It is critical to become equipped with the essential knowledge and understanding of different cultures, practices, beliefs, governmental governance and procedures.

How can you gain knowledge and understanding? Daphne Tan-Chin provides these helpful tips from her work in process, *International Culture and Today's Marketplace.*

- **Research.** Surf the country's official website where you will learn demographic, economic and resource information. While there are ample materials online, visit your local library as well.
- **Visit embassies and consulates.** Identify natives who are willing to share their cultural practices and knowledge.
- **Participate in associations and clubs functions,** mingle with the country's citizens; this is another excellent way to learn and adapt to the culture.
- **Develop a tolerance for foreign practices.** Your practices and beliefs may seem as ridiculous as theirs are to you. Keep an open mind and adapt to the different approaches, beliefs and practices.
- **Compromise if at all possible.** Some practices may conflict with yours. Learn to compromise or negotiate to come to an ultimate agreement. Compromising is a positive attribute to many cultures of the world. It is not regarded as a weakness.
- **Ask if uncertain.** Do not assume that because your method has not been objected, it is agreeable with all. When doing business with other citizens, it is advisable to minimize offensive or undesirable methods. An acceptable way to recognize if there may be a problem is to subtly bring the issue up and look for nonverbal cues. Nonverbal expressions are give aways for detecting inconsistencies. In some cultures, it is considered rude to bluntly give a negative answer to a question; it is acceptable for the party to agree or divert an answer to avoid a negative confrontation.
- **Patience.** A virtue in many cultures is seen as deteriorating trait in the American culture. Since we are always on the move with a million things

to complete in 24 hours our lives are governed by instantaneous actions and reactions. There is a deadline for every aspect of our lives - business and personal. We leave work at a certain time to get our children to their after school activities. Most of us go without lunch at work to meet our deadlines. Business meetings are conducted at the lunch hours. Global businesses and relationships are "delicately prepared" to obtain the desired "taste." Many cultures consider time an essence to life. It takes time to develop a solidly trusting relationship; a good business partner is based on the strength of this relationship.

Global Marketplace Web Sites

Research global marketplace web sites. Go to your search engine and plug in global marketplace and you will find page after page of specific sites that will help you obtain more information about the fascinating world of the global village.

Keeping in mind that the world is becoming the new economic melting pot, consider the following as you think globally. See the Appendix for more global web sites.

Thinking Points for Connecting Forward

- Open yourself to the vast amount of opportunities when you think globally.
- Every country has a cultural influence that will impact your relationship.
- Think about the information critical for a successful global partnership.
- Develop an in-depth understanding of the culture that your global partner comes from.
- Research, research, research!

Chapter 18

Summary

This vast playing field is exciting and has great potential. This strategy has stressed the critical importance of looking at global endeavors intellectually, researching and securing professional and legal advice along the way. As you develop your global expertise, the questions you ask as you go forward are vitally important. Talking to others who have developed global partnerships will also help you learn through their hard earned lessons.

Take a walk down memory lane with Strategy Fourteen, and Look Back to Move Forward.

> *An individual-friendly global marketplace is possible: one that realizes the great potential for all of our citizens.*
>
> **Mozelle W. Thompson, Commissioner**
> United States Federal Trade Commission

Chapter 19

Strategy Fourteen

Look Back to Move Forward: *Taking the Moment & Dancing with It*

> *Human relationships always help us to carry on because they always presuppose further developments, a future, and also because we live as if our only task was precisely to have relationships with other people.*
>
> **Albert Camus,** French-Algerian Philosopher and Writer

Ron: While I have always felt I understood the value of relationship with others, it was not until we started writing this book that my realization that relationships do not have to end was reinforced.

Let me take a few moments to share this experience with you. The times in my life that I have always treasured are my teenage years. During those years, I sought to find my way in life, formulate my values, and adapt the character of the person I was to become.

Almost all of the people that I met or spent time with during my adolescence had an impact in shaping my future. From a musical perspective, it was The Beatles and the Beach Boys. And then, there were the friendships.

Have you ever thought about the impact of your best friend, your best friend of the opposite sex, and your first boyfriend or girlfriend? What makes them so special? Well, in my opinion, what makes them so special is what you *attach* to the experiences you had with them. For me, it was a time of discovery, a time of experiment, and a time of questioning: truly my wonder years.

In October of 2002, I reconnected with two people from my high school years: my best female friend and my first love from the 60s. Wow!

After a series of e-mails and phone conversations, the three of us decided to get together for an extended 4-day weekend in beautiful South Florida in late February.

We hardly missed a beat from the last time we were all together in 1967. From that time, we've continued to connect.

What am I really saying or suggesting? I'm suggesting you think about the meaningful relationships you had in the past. Then ask yourself the following question. If I were to reconnect with these people today, is it possible that I would have satisfying and joyful experiences?

If you once connected so powerfully, chances are you would again. The renewed friendship could be very exciting, and enjoyable, and continue into the future.

We have said throughout this book that relationships never end. And why should they? Relationships play such an important part in everyone's life. Each relationship is such a precious commodity; renewing and shifting these relationships into the future opens up undiscovered possibilities.

Perhaps as you look back, some relationships were filled with too much conflict, too many hang-ups and so on and so on. Having a positive response may be your guidepost.

Search out and start the process of rebuilding those incredible relationships you loved from the past. Enjoy the process of taking yesteryear's relationships and bringing them into the present. In essence, you're looking back in order to move ahead.

Taking the Moment & Dancing With It

Taking the moment and dancing with it is a term I first learned in 1974. I was a bass player seeking to align with an upcoming band in Los Angeles. I responded to an ad for a singing bass player by two gentlemen building a musical theme around their book, *The Awakening: The Electromagnetic Spectrum.* They were Robert Bearns and Ron Dexter.

Robert was somewhat of a philosopher and would always point out the need to take the moment. He would go on to state that people often move quickly past opportunities for mutual success. He also stated that if you want to know or understand more, all you need to do is take the moment and notice more.

How true it is. Taking the time to notice more, and know again the people we have enjoyed being with in the past allows for movement into our forward thinking future. It's the experience of *relationshift* that Jane introduced earlier: the act of identifying and transforming your thoughts and your view of a relationship into a new relationship. Relationshift truly works!

By the way, we recorded a few albums while together: The Golden Voyage music series by Bearns and Dexter, Awakening Productions, Culver City, California.

Thinking Points for Connecting Forward

- Take a walk down memory lane. What are the relationships that you've experienced that you truly enjoyed? What would it take to reach out and reestablish contact with these individuals? What resistances do you have? What support do you need to contact these individuals?
- Remember a relationship that once was has the possibility to shift into a relationship now and move into the future.
- Taking the moment and dancing with it is possible for today's relationships, and for yesterday's as well.

Summary

Taking the moment and dancing with it is truly an art. Going back in time and rediscovering connections from the past, you're doing just that. Look up someone from your past, and "notice" if there is a shift possible for a new relationship to emerge. To support your efforts in finding some of those wonderful relationships you had in the past, Part Three notes additional recommendations and website resources that will support your search and reconnection opportunities. Enjoy!

You are about to join us in Strategy 15, the final strategy that is not final at all! Applying this strategy will launch you on a continual journey and spiral of a lifetime of revival in all aspects of your life.

> *The relationship is the communication bridge between people.*
>
> **Alfred Kadushin**

Strategy Fifteen

Continuous Learning with Purpose: *Ongoing Enhancement of Life Through Personal and Professional Growth*

Chapter 20

> *Personal mastery goes beyond competence and skills, though it is grounded in competence and skills. It goes beyond spiritual unfolding or opening, although it requires spiritual growth. It means approaching one's life as a creative work.*
>
> **Peter Senge,** *The Fifth Discipline*

Jane: Learning and unlearning from past successes and challenges is a life long process! We continuously learn new skills, new ways of thinking, new technology, new business strategies, new information, new self knowledge, new management and leadership thought. We believe that is it so important and so daunting that we are focusing this entire strategy on providing a process for lifetime learning that connects to purpose. Strategy one, we began with your relationship with self, where you determined that which is most important to you. This last strategy returns your focus once again on you, and on your own growth and development.

This strategy integrates the three relationship themes not stated but woven throughout this book:

- **Spiritual** (relationship with a higher force)
- **Intrapersonal** (relationship with self)
- **Interpersonal** (relationship with others)

This process takes you to the next level of continuous learning along an upward and deepening spiral of growth and development. Central questions guide this process. While your own questions will emerge, here are examples that may serve you along the continuous learning cycle.

Does this choice enhance your purpose in life?

Does this doing reflect your purpose and intentions?

Does this relationship enhance your life?

Is this relationship mutually rewarding?

Does this learning reflect your purpose and intentions?

As you *learn forward,* reflect on your intentions for a whole, healthy, and happy life. For example:

- Balance of Personal and Professional Life
- Emotional and Intellectual Well-being (Nourishing Mind, Body, Spirit)
- Career and Professional Health
- Physical Health, Exercise, and Diet
- Creativity and Re-creation

Getting in step with growth and development in all dimensions of your life puts you in touch with your capacity for continuous learning. Growth is defined here as expanding potential. It is the awareness of where you've been and an integration of personal and professional insights and skills that improve your effectiveness now. Growth is the awareness of all those choice moments along your way.

Tom Peters, business consultant and author, encourages cultivating towering competence, honing new skills and capabilities. Here is another image to consider: cultivating a deepening spiral of continuous learning which takes one back to a focal point from start to finish. While you are honing new skills and capabilities, you are mindful of aligning your skill set choices and considering the impact of those choices on the many intentions you have for your life. You come from one focal point, living your life purposefully.

Your Focal Point

Imagine for a moment this focal point: your purpose. As you move from your purpose into continuous learning, you make choices that progressively lead you forward. Upward and around, you return once again to the same intentional point on the spiral, yet at a potentially more fulfilled, competent, confident state. Returning to your purpose and your questions, you once again choose that which is nourishing and life enhancing for the "whole" of you. The following is a visual illustration developed by me and Phil Black showing how alignment to purpose takes place.

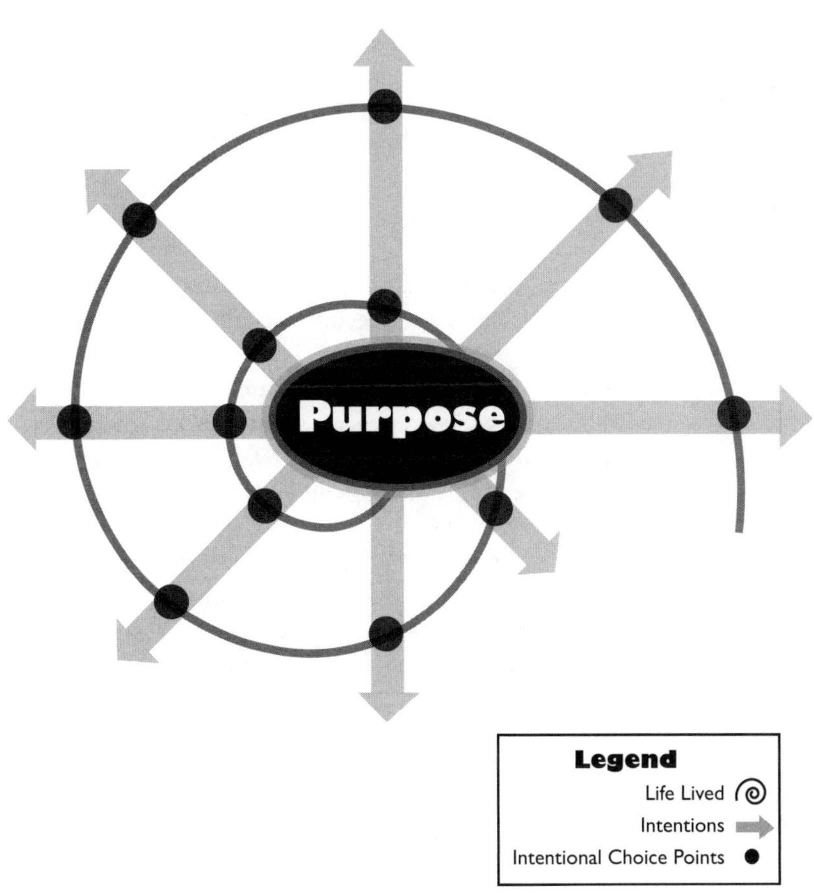

Spiral of Growth and Development:
A model to visualize life's continual journey

Key Points

- Purpose is focal point at core of spiral for "whole" life. You must first determine your purpose.
- As you establish intentions for your life, ask yourself if the intention aligns with your purpose.
- Life intention lines move from purpose: Family, Career, Education, Health, Sports, etc.
- Intentional moments are points on the spiral where lines intersect with spiral: These are choice points.
- Identify questions at these junctures that align with intention and help you discern what next action to take (i.e., considering taking a course, or embarking on a degree program, or spending a weekend at a personal growth retreat.) Does this choice align with your intention?
- Going into action, you experience your choice and make modifications along the way correcting misalignments as they occur.
- At completion, you return once again to intentional point where you reflect on lessons learned, evaluate successes and challenges, and examine conditioning or relationship habits that no longer serve you. You let go and unlearn thinking that no longer enhances your life.
- Each time you come around the spiral and meet up with the intentional point, you are coming back with more life lived, and hopefully deepened growth and development.
- You are continuously beginning again and again.

Developed by Jane George-Surges and Phil Black

There's a very subtle, basic, and underlying component at the core of this spiral, which creates balance and quality in one's entire life, and that is discernment.

Discernment

In the book, *The Art of Possibility* by Rosamund Stone Zander and Benjamin Zander, the authors refer to the musicians of the New York Philharmonic Orchestra who were asked to name their all time most effective conductor. Arturo Tocanini was chosen. When asked why, one of the musicians said, "he could anticipate when you were about to make a mistake and keep you from making it." That is one way to describe discernment.

Discernment is the ability to make an aligned decision, to grasp and comprehend what is not immediately obvious. It is the power to distinguish and select what is most appropriate. Applied through astute observation skills such as Arturo Tocanini demonstrates, you make the adjustment that is needed precisely as it is needed. That is using continuous learning in the present, letting go of what may have worked previously to discern what is needed in this moment. Now, take a look a little further out into the future. As you look ahead at goals and objectives that are set, discern what knowledge, information, skills, education is need. Through discernment, choose that which reflects the direction you intend your life to take. Here are four principles to help you toward continuous learning.

The First Principle of Continuous Learning: *Process Knowledge Versus Content Knowledge*

With a vast amount of content knowledge, educational programs, and a menu of skills to choose from, where do you start? We emphasize purpose as the touchstone for decision making; your choices come from purpose. Once you start there, you must still look at two factors: process and content. In previous decades, content was king. You were rewarded in school systems with the highest grade when you could demonstrate retention of a vast amount of information. Now, in school systems and in the work place, it is the process of gathering and generating information, working with others, and creating relationships that is most transforming. Understanding process, how your own process works, and how you work in relationship is paramount. Your process will also include the ability to discern. You will constantly discern and choose what is most aligned to your purpose, that which is most important to you.

Chapter 20

The Second Principle of Continuous Learning: *Maximizing the Ability to Learn*

This principle focuses on the process of learning. This process learning approach integrates eight learning intelligences developed by Howard Gardner, Professor in Cognition and Education, Harvard Graduate School. You will increase your ability to learn when you are able to discern which method to choose in a given situation. While you will have more then one preference, your favorite learning process may be the one that is the most natural fit for you.

Learning Intelligences

- **Visual/Spatial:** Through a visual and spatial process, images, drawings, sketches, maps, charts, pictures, puzzles, designs, films, charts, pictures, puzzles, designs, films, videos, visualization, and imagination help you strengthen your ability to retain and apply your learning.

- **Logical/Mathematical:** Through a logical and mathematical process, reasoning, deductive and inductive logic, facts, data, spreadsheets, databases, sequencing, ranking, analyzing, judging, evaluations, assessments are tools that help you retain and apply your learning.

- **Verbal/Linguistic:** Through the process of speaking, writing, listening, reading, papers, essays, poems, plays, narratives, memos, bulletins, newspapers, e-mails, faxes, dialogues, and debates, you are better able to digest your learning, retain the learning, and apply.

- **Music/Rhythmic:** Through music, tones, and rhythm, you are naturally drawn to use beat, melody, tunes, choir, rap, ads, or jingles in learning and interfacing with others.

- **Bodily/Kinesthetic:** Through activity, motion, action, experiment, hands-on, acting out dramas or role plays, disassemble, reassemble, touch, feel, and other experiential processes, you are better able to experience and retain the learning. It is through the act of doing and application, that you best absorb and integrate new skills.

- **Interpersonal/Social:** Through interactive gatherings with others in groups or one-on-one, you strengthen your ability to learn through conversing, sharing, or "chewing up" information, facts, or data. Through this process you strengthen your understanding in the process.

- **Intra-personal/Introspective:** Through solitude, meditation, and reflection, you are able to envision, plot, plan, dream, write, goal-set, and analyze your own ideas to then integrate with the learning resources that you have received from others.

- **Naturalist:** Through listening, watching, observing, classifying, categorizing, and discerning patterns, you see systems and better learn and unlearn, letting go of that which no longer works. You are pulled toward living things, lakes, rivers, water falls and see the connection between eco systems and human systems.

As Gardner implies, the more fluidly we understand the different types of learning intelligences, the better we understand that there is no "right" way to learn. There are many ways to integrate learning to heighten comprehension of various concepts, knowledge and skills. Diagnosing the learning tools that are available and choosing the one or ones that may better help in a given situation is your discerning challenge. You can apply this process approach to learning intelligences with someone you are living with, teaching, parenting or when you are simply seeking to find a bridge to another.

As a teacher and consultant, I am better able to understand the ways in which my students learn. Thus, the more students know about their own learning styles and the host of other ways of learning, and the more I understand the dynamics of learning, the more able we are to partner in the learning, comprehension, and application process. The same is true in every environment.

Chapter 20

The Third Principle of Continuous Learning: *Diagnosing and Learning Forward*

To continuously discern, you do not decide to become a plumber when you are wanting to understand the basics of operating your sink. You do not need to become an electrician to use the hair dryer.

- What are the expert skills and competence levels to move you toward the success you've imagined?
- What knowledge aligns with goals and objectives?
- What Just-in-Time (JIT) and Expert Knowledge helps along the way?

Focusing your continuous learning on your current profession, and related disciplines, as well as exploring other career directions, keeps you learning and fuels your learning forward. It was long ago said that we will have five, six or more careers in a lifetime. Multiple careers co-exist. Teaching, consult/coaching, training and development, and writing are four distinct careers paths that I am developing, with project subsets under each. Look around and see if you are finding that for yourself and for others.

The Fourth Principle of Continuous Learning: *Ongoing Identification of Support and Resources*

Along the way, you will have many choice points as well as many challenges. A question to ask yourself at these junctures: what support and what resources do you need in order to take the next step? The support of others is key to your continuous learning success. As we've said earlier, we have not gotten to this point in time without the help of others. We must remember this as we go forward. We are interdependent beings and as we ask others for help, we are better able to give back and help others along their way. We must also make conscious decisions to be open to teachers we meet along our path.

Thinking Points for Connecting Forward

- Look for a focused direction in all aspects of your life, as you discern forward. Suspend logic and reach for creativity to make up something new. Logic, facts, and information are not to be solely relied on, but are helpful tools within the discerning process.
- Develop the ability to diagnose: What is Needed Now?

Summary

Using this model as a framework for continuous learning, you see how it is possible to cultivate a deepening spiraling process of growth and development. Here is a quick review of this strategy. Determine your purpose. Your purpose gives you a touchstone to go back to time and time again. Develop your ability to discern. Discernment will help you as you choose and learn forward. Use the four principles of continuous learning. First understand process knowledge versus being content driven. Second, understand your preferred learning style and a host of learning intelligences to diagnose and utilize as you develop new competencies and skills. Third, use the concept of learning forward: what are the skills now, what knowledge aligns with goals and objectives, and what JITK and expert knowledge needs to be accessed? Fourth, reach out and get help along the way. It is a great strength to ask for help, resources, and support in all areas of our lives, and to say yes to the many teachers who come along in their many shapes, sizes, and forms.

This entire strategy provides a process for you to tap into your greater vitality and intelligence. Doing so, you move toward ongoing enhancement of all dimensions of your life.

This strategy caps off Part Two. We are at the edge of this new understanding of relationships as the core in the business world. Rich and complex, focusing on relationships as the primary organizing force will change your world, and is world-changing.

Now begin Part Three where you will find worksheets, questions, and guidelines to help you apply the fifteen strategies.

The transformation of the human being requires something more - it can only be achieved if there is a "real meeting" between the conscious force which descends and the total commitment that answers it.

George Gurdjieff (1877-1949)

Part Three
Bringing It All Together

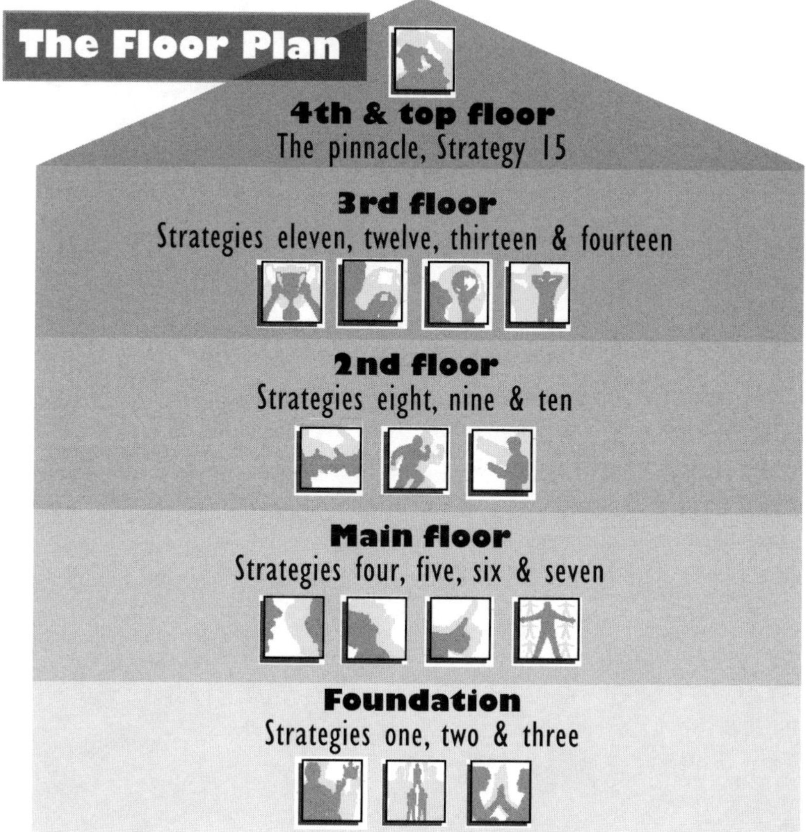

PART THREE
BRINGING IT ALL TOGETHER

Chapter 21

In Part Three, you now choose from your vantage point the strategy to guide you as you reflect on the specific relationship in front of you. This process is at the core of NetBeing, the word coined to capture the essence of a relationship mindset. The specific steps, worksheets and guidelines will help you put the fifteen relationship strategies to work for you and establish an organized plan of action. In addition, at the end of each strategy, you will be provided space to integrate these skills through action steps.

Action steps captured at the end of each strategy will propel you forward. Note these actions steps on your calendar to continue the momentum.

Strategy One
Live Life Purposefully:
The Relationship Within

Purpose

Although each strategy stands alone, there is a link that threads throughout: purpose. This link begins with the first strategy and is your invitation to look inward to discover and uncover what is most important to you. In this first strategy you focus on self awareness and identifying your purpose, the touchstone for you to return to time and time again as you live life purposefully. You also identify intentions for yourself that reflect the whole of your life. Now is the time to move into action.

Cultivate Your Ability to Understand Your Purpose

- Go to school on yourself.
- Use your intuition.
- Understand your gut feelings. What are they telling you?
- How would you like to live your life?
- What has been a common theme over your lifetime? For example for Jane it is to develop holistically and to full potential and to help others do the same. For Ron, it is to make connections with others in the world, and to help others do the same.

Record your intentions. Here are several examples: Writer, Mother, Key Note Speaker, Teacher, Coach, Consultant, Healthy Life Style, Friend, or Husband.

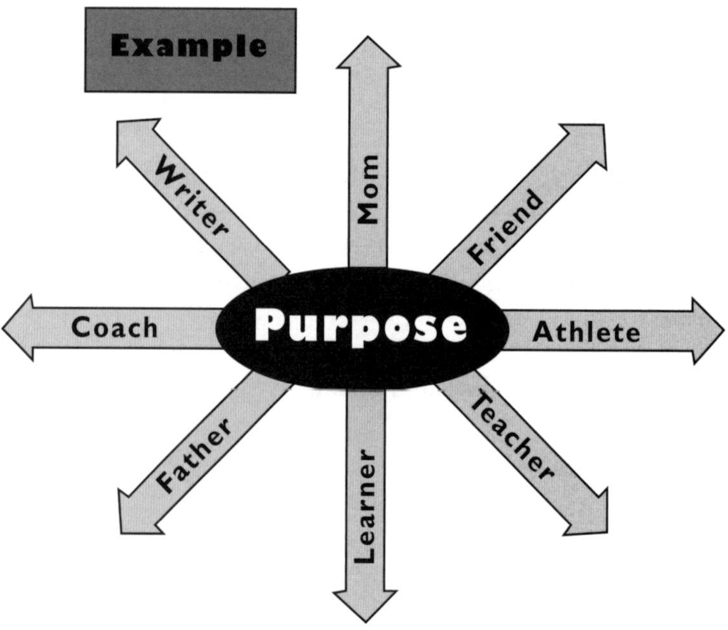

Your Intentions

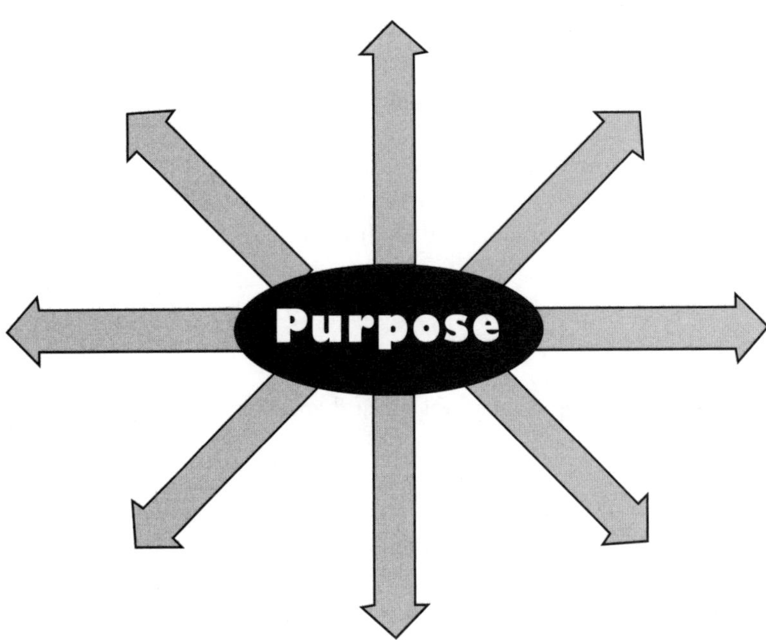

Linking Intention to Planning & Goal Setting

Now begin the planning process. Goals develop naturally from purpose and intention. For example, if your purpose is to bring laughter and joy into peoples' lives, your intention may be to start a business where enjoyment and laughter is a part of your business plan.

To help you in your goal setting, consider the following:

- Scan the horizon. What is going on around you?
- Study the work of futurists. How can you meet the emerging needs of future generations? It has been said that in the next ten years, new career paths will be spawned that are currently beyond the comprehension of the everyday person. What could they be?
- Where is the work that needs doing?
- What are the unmet needs of those around you?
- How is change creating new opportunities while current or previous opportunities are fading away?
- Develop group discussions around areas where you need input from others.
- Scan books, management reports, magazines and trade papers.
- Speak with opinion leaders in the community.
- What time frames or windows of opportunity are you facing?
- Who and what resources would help you?
- What are the new qualifications that you need to possess?

(Consider what William Bridges says in his book *Jobshift* *"...new qualifications exist inside of us rather then on our resumes."*)

Planning and Goal Setting

State goal clearly in writing. ______________________________

____

How does it align to purpose? ____________________________

____

Why is this project important in other ways? ________________

____

What is its impact on me and others? ______________________

____

Who will need to be involved? ____________________________

____

How will I accomplish this goal? __________________________

____

What financial resources will I need? ______________________

____

How will I know if I am successful? ______________________

____

Now, it's yours turn to record your goals and objectives that connect to your intentions.

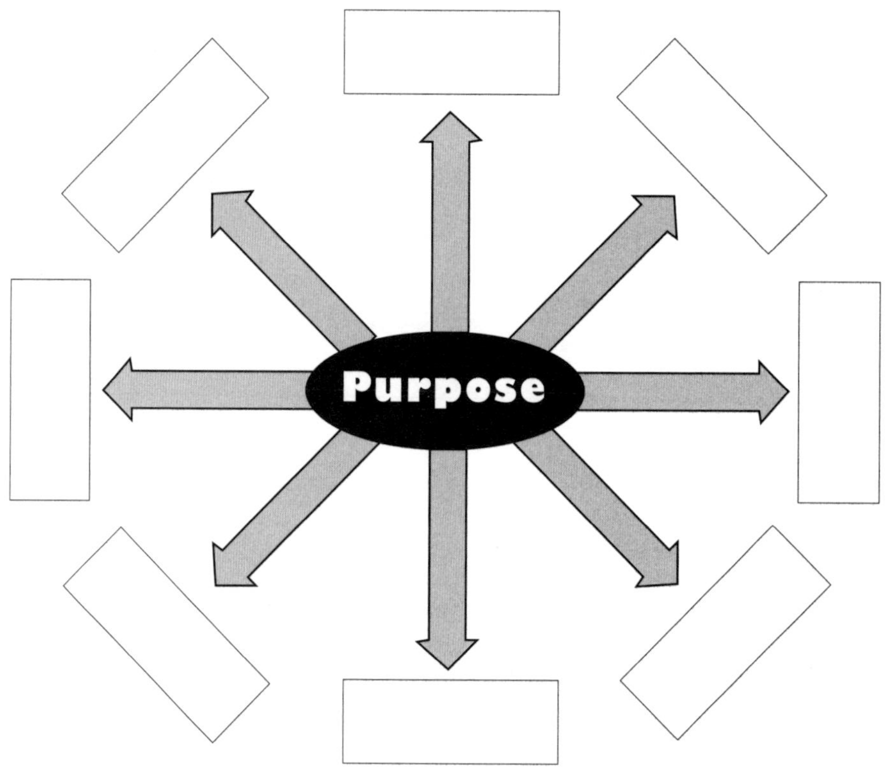

Questions to Guide Self-Reflection

1. What goals need to be put into place in order to meet your intentions?
2. How does your goal align to your vision?
3. Are you compromising yourself at all or sacrificing other parts of your life to accomplish your goal?
4. What is the impact of the goals on you and others?
5. Who will need to be involved?
6. How will you go about meeting and developing relationships to help you achieve success?
7. What actions steps do you need to take?
8. Are you considering what you really want at this point in your life?

Action Steps

- Create a budget.
- Prepare a time estimate.
- List and contact key individuals who will be important to this objective.
- Confirm plans in advance.

Chapter 21

Leadership With Purpose

As a leader, your ability to project intention and vision helps team members in their ability to be creative and develop an organizational presence. With this shared focus, people around you are better able to align with each other and more effortlessly accomplish objectives.

In their much-referenced book *Leaders: The Strategy for Taking Charge,* Warren Bennis and Burt Nanus promote the importance of vision in leaders. They say, "By focusing attention on a vision, the leader operates on the emotional and spiritual resources of people around them." Take this one step further. Others who possess a passion and direction for their life inspire individuals and the work they are led to perform. People are influenced by those who have a passion for life, who live with purpose and intention, and who possess a freedom not merely to see possibilities, but who commit and take positive action in their life.

Internal Contents

Let's go back for a moment to understand internal contents. Internal contents contain history, conditioning, thinking patterns, socialization and multiple other factors. How comfortable are you with change? Are you comfortable with risk? How do you handle conflict? What values have you accumulated over your life time? Perhaps you want to weed some of them out if they are no longer working for you. We ask you to learn as much about yourself as possible, what resistances you have, as well as what motivates you.

As you move toward alignment to purpose, watch for those internal contents which may become internal constraints.

	Internal Contents	Internal Constraints	Awareness of "Work"
EXAMPLE	Worry	Reluctant to take risk	Identify underlying fears

Now, get ready, set, aim and record your mission, goals, and beliefs as it pertains to global partnering. Ron sets the tone by sharing his mission, intentions, and beliefs.

MISSION

Ron: The mission of a Global Partner is to promote the exchange of business and personal opportunities among professional, quality conscious people.

I will conduct my business and life with integrity, and in a manner consistent with the highest quality standards of all Global Partners around the world.

Your Mission

INTENTIONS

Ron: To be one of the most productive, innovative and committed Global Partners in my community as measured by participation and results.

To build my NetBeing system on traditions of integrity, reliability and commitment.

Your Intention

GOALS

Ron: To obtain feedback from my network on an ongoing basis, since meeting and exceeding my partner's expectations is the foundation of my NetBeing commitment.

To expand my NetBeing system to attain a significant presence in the community in which I live and work.

To evaluate my achievements using traditional and innovative measurements.

Your Goals

BELIEFS

Ron: To fulfill my NetBeing mission and achieve my goals, I will build my networking future on the following:

- ***I believe...*** that **Net***Being* associates are my first priority and that one hundred percent participation is the key to my success. For my system to succeed, I recognize that the more I know about others, the more likely I can help them. Meeting and exceeding the expectations of my network is a prerequisite for facilitating network interaction.

- ***I believe...*** that the people in my network make the difference. Because my success depends on the quality of people coming into my system, personal selection is a critical quality decision. To attract and retain the best people, I will continue to innovate and create an environment that will support successful business and personal interaction. I will offer informative and challenging discussions, and personal growth opportunities.

- ***I believe...*** in the Givers Gain Philosophy of doing business. The more business I can generate for others, the greater success I will have in reaching my goals. My work will be predicated on the concept of "what goes around, comes around." If I freely give to others, I will receive business freely as well.

- ***I believe...*** that every colleague has a stake in my success or failure. We are partners in a **Net***Being* system. As in any partnership, there must be trust and open communication throughout my system.

- ***I believe...*** that my **Net***Being* system is for business people who mean business. I realize that we're linked together by common goals and we are encouraged to share ideas, information, and resources. It has been proven time and time again that by helping others get to where they are going, we can truly experience the real meaning of success.

- ***I believe...*** that **Net***Being as a way of life,* will change my whole way of doing business. As a technique, it will introduce me to knowledgeable allies I didn't know I had. As a process, it knows no limits and neither will I if I use it to its fullest potential.

- ***I believe...*** that innovation is critical to achieving quality results. Successful **Net***Being* systems will be those that anticipate and quickly adapt to change. I am determined to devote resources to the development of new ideas that will provide better methods for networking interaction. When innovative proposals show potential, I will be committed to acting on them promptly.

- ***I believe...*** that leadership is the key responsibility of those who want to build a successful **Net***Being* system. I believe that superior organizational performance is achieved when a spirit of teamwork, enthusiasm and commitment exists. I will be accountable for achieving results and for fostering a climate that encourages people to give their best effort.

- ***I believe...*** that integrity and fair dealing must be at the heart of every business decision I make. A tradition of, and reputation for, ethical behavior is of paramount importance to my **Net***Being* system family of associates. I will treat others who I meet for the first time with fairness and good faith, and I expect of myself and others honesty, integrity, and compliance with values and ethics of the highest standing.

- ***I believe...*** in serving the community; devoted to the common good, continuing a tradition of providing information, support and services that promote health, education and quality of life.

- ***I believe...*** in the entrepreneurial spirit. I will foster this spirit among others because innovation, self-expression and prudent risk taking will provide me with a competitive advantage, and will provide my **Net***Being* system with what it takes to be the best we can be.

Now, your turn:

I believe: ____________________

As you consider this strategy, what action steps will you take? Add these steps to your calendar right now.

Strategy Two

Develop a Relationship Mindset:

Becoming a Relationship Builder

While various combinations of interpersonal skills, focus and commitment have been proven to accelerate the relationship building process, they can only be effective if we understand how we currently operate and how we currently think. How we think impacts what we do in relationship. Albert Einstein said, *"The world that we have made as a result of the level of thinking we have done thus far creates problems that we cannot solve at the same level of thinking at which we created them."*

Chapter 21

This strategy emphasizes the importance of fostering an attitude of mind toward building solid long lasting relationships with others. We also focus on the foundational principle of commitment to a relationship approach, providing descriptions to help you see where you are and where you would like to be. Following is an assessment to help reveal your level of relationship skills based on your current mindset.

Assessing your Relationship Mindset Quotient

1 I listen intently to another person, deeply caring about their personal happiness outside of my own.

Usually ☐ Frequently ☐ Sometimes ☐ Rarely ☐

2 I work toward mutually rewarding outcomes when working on a project with another.

Usually ☐ Frequently ☐ Sometimes ☐ Rarely ☐

3 I know what is important to me and focus my intention toward meeting the individuals that align with my vision.

Usually ☐ Frequently ☐ Sometimes ☐ Rarely ☐

4 I try and build relationships when I experience a connection and mutuality for short term and long term objectives.

Usually ☐ Frequently ☐ Sometimes ☐ Rarely ☐

5 I focus on developing relationships over time that meet long term goals and objectives.

Usually ☐ Frequently ☐ Sometimes ☐Rarely ☐

6 I often make the most of the relationships I develop by determining what is important to the other as well as to myself.

Usually ☐ Frequently ☐ Sometimes ☐ Rarely ☐

7 I look for opportunities to start a relationship as often as I can.

Usually ☐ Frequently ☐ Sometimes ☐ Rarely ☐

8 I trust my instincts and take the initiative in meeting new people in multiple ways.

Usually ☐ Frequently ☐ Sometimes ☐ Rarely ☐

9 I seek productive and creative ways to relationship satisfaction.

Usually ☐ Frequently ☐ Sometimes ☐ Rarely ☐

10 I link one relationship to another.

Usually ☐ Frequently ☐ Sometimes ☐ Rarely ☐

11 I keep my relationship building philosophy consistent.

Usually ☐ Frequently ☐ Sometimes ☐ Rarely ☐

12 I am willing to be vulnerable and inform the other when the relationship is trending negatively, or when we have difficult issues to discuss.

Usually ☐ Frequently ☐ Sometimes ☐ Rarely ☐

13 I develop a plan of action in building my relationships and finding support.

Usually ☐ Frequently ☐ Sometimes ☐ Rarely ☐

14 I obtain agreement for the joint actions discussed to minimize confusion about expectations.

Usually ☐ Frequently ☐ Sometimes ☐ Rarely ☐

15 I work with and develop teams of people to move projects to completion.

Usually ☐ Frequently ☐ Sometimes ☐ Rarely ☐

16 I am careful to avoid unfulfilled expectations of others, and talk about how projects are going.

Usually ☐ Frequently ☐ Sometimes ☐ Rarely ☐

17 I seek opportunities to reward, celebrate and encourage relationships.

Usually ☐ Frequently ☐ Sometimes ☐ Rarely ☐

18 I make sure that each interaction is working toward a triple win outcome.

Usually ☐ Frequently ☐ Sometimes ☐ Rarely ☐

19 I anticipate where conflict may arise, and plan how to respond through a conflict resolution mindset.

Usually ☐ Frequently ☐ Sometimes ☐ Rarely ☐

20 I share my knowledge, information and resources with others freely.

Usually ☐ Frequently ☐ Sometimes ☐ Rarely ☐

21 When I feel defensive, I identify my feelings and respond in a way that is authentic while proactively looking for a bridge to the other.

Usually ☐ Frequently ☐ Sometimes ☐ Rarely ☐

22 I enjoy meeting both like-minded people and people who think differently than I do.

Usually ☐ Frequently ☐ Sometimes ☐ Rarely ☐

23 My behavior is flexible and highly adaptable to people's needs.

Usually ☐ Frequently ☐ Sometimes ☐ Rarely ☐

24 I encourage people to speak their minds openly and to share their concerns, and have good follow-up measures in place, encouraging ongoing feedback.

Usually ☐ Frequently ☐ Sometimes ☐ Rarely ☐

25 I focus on delivering my best effort, believing in developing quality relationships.

Usually ☐ Frequently ☐ Sometimes ☐ Rarely ☐

Key: Assign point breakdowns as follows: Usually: 4 points each; Frequently: 3 points each; Sometimes: 2 points each; Rarely: 1 point each

Analysis

After completing this self-assessment, add your total score to determine your mindset level. Regardless of your level, it is important to remember that we can always improve.

28-55: If your desire isto increase your level of relationship, reevaluate what you are currently doing and seize every opportunity to practice the relationship strategies.

56-78: You understand what it takes to build strong relationships with others. Keep strengthening your approach and continue to seek to support the efforts of others.

79-91: You are a natural at creating relationships with others. Remember that relationships are always changing. Continue to better understand the changes that others go through and assess current needs and opportunities.

92-100: You have taken your relationship mindset to an extraordinary level.

Total possible score is: 100 points

Jane: From my personal experience and my work in relationship coaching, it has become very clear that our characteristics are constantly changing in interaction with one other person. To illustrate this, I am using Human Cells as a metaphor to illustrate character traits. A cell is the simplest unit of living matter *working together with trillions of other cells in an organized manner for the benefit of the total being.*

Like human cells, all of the diverse characteristics that make up one human being are beyond comprehension. Like cells that participate in who we are physiologically, our characteristics also participate together to make up how we show up in relationship! The composition and number of cells constantly change as cells fall off and new ones are created. The same is true for character traits. They constantly change or *fall away* in relationship to another person, situation, and the environment.

It is the intention of this strategy to help you think about character traits that work together in an *organized manner for the benefit of the relationship;* become aware of characteristics that are not helpful to the relationship, and those that are.

This is what this illustration points to. What are your characteristics? Good or bad, uncovering these traits will help you see yourself better. Many of these characteristics are hidden. You heighten your awareness of them in relationship. When a relationship is trending negatively, when you are triggered, when you feel competitive with another, when you are told you are not trusted, or when you do not trust another--these are opportunities to discover hidden character traits. It is up to you to develop your ability to bring to light character traits that are surfacing.

Like human cells that fall off, the death of a character trait may occur when you find you no longer need it. Perhaps in the past, you have valued competitiveness as a character trait. While there is nothing wrong with healthy competition, you may be finding that the competitive trait is not useful to you if you are truly working toward the benefit of another or the mutual benefit of the relationship. Perhaps you are finding that there is a character trait that you do not possess that would be beneficial to the relationship. What is it? Simply heightening your awareness of this character trait may help you form or bring it forward.

If you are forming a relationship or partnership only for financial gain and your own personal success, it will be very challenging for you to obtain *relationship* success and impossible to reach a mutual outcome.

Saying this from another angle--some experts on character might tell you what characteristics you "should" possess. The objective here is to help you amplify your existing characteristics and help you simply see yourself better in relationship. Think about a relationship that is not working so well right now. What character traits are surfacing for you in relationship with this person? Now, think about a relationship that is working very well. What character traits are surfacing for you in relationship with this person? This ongoing stepping back, and observing or witnessing yourself in relationship, will heighten your awareness of self and help you mindfully choose the character trait or traits most beneficial to the relationship. And, will help you to do your personal work as you watch patterns of behavior or traits over time that get in the way of relationship, and, or guide you to step away from the relationship.

Important characteristics of a relationship mindset

- **ATTENTIVE:** You pay attention to the relational needs and respond accordingly. From dressing for the proper occasion to listening three times as much, you attend to what is necessary in the moment.
- **RESPONSIVENESS:** Provides prompt response or communicates challenges and or delays in a timely manner.
- **ASSURANCE:** Demonstrate your expertise, and communicate areas where you are not an expert. Identify and or recommend other experts when needed to help you to deliver the quality product or service.
- **EMPATHY:** Listening to the needs, emotions, and challenges and finding understanding within you of the other person's perspective and situation.
- **DISCERNMENT:** Choose actions based on your ability to determine and distinguish that which is "right" or appropriate based on all the factors at hand. The ability to sort through many variables to grasp and comprehend what is not readily obvious or visible.
- **Interact with VULNERABILITY** and appropriate **DISCLOSURE.**
- **Demonstrate INTERPERSONAL skills** that fosters acceptance and partnership.
- **CONTINUOUS LEARNING** by attending workshops, seminars, discussion groups to improve skills and self performance; always learning.
- **FOCUSED on HELPING** others and receiving help.
- **Provide GUIDANCE** to others.
- **SHARE** knowledge eagerly.
- **Make REFERRALS** with no intention of personal rewards back to you.

Identify relationships that would be better served if you intentionally brought different traits into the relationship. As you reflect on this strategy, what action steps will you take to further your understanding of your character and apply traits to a specific relationship? Add these steps to your calendar right now.

____

____

____

____

____

____

Strategy Three

Declare Your Interdependence & Cooperation: *Your Independence is a Direct Result*

In Part Two, we emphasized the importance of seeing self as interdependent; we have always and we will always need each other to be successful. We see how our interdependence strengthens the ability to be independent. Interdependence ultimately results in liberation: the ability to be self sufficient, and to contribute to the world. We now provide questions to help you assess how your interdependence and cooperation play out in various relationships. As you read the following questions, think about a relationship with which you are currently struggling.

1 **Trust:** Do I trust you and do you trust me to follow through? Do I trust that you will tell me when you are unable to help me? Do I trust that you will keep confidential concerns to yourself? Do I trust you to tell me when things aren't working? Do I trust that you will work through learning curves with me?

2 **Mutual Vulnerability:** Do I feel safe to share struggles, concerns, misgivings, with you? Do I feel safe that we can work through the tough times or go our separate ways without incrimination? Are you willing to be vulnerable with me: sharing your struggles, concerns, misgivings with me?

3 **Mutuality:** Do I see mutuality in our relationship? Do I see how I can help you and you can help me? Do I see that we can positively impact each other through shared learning, through sharing contacts, through providing services to one another, through friendship and/or support?

4 **Respect:** Do I respect you and feel respected by you? Do we show consideration for each other beyond the work that we are doing together? Is there positive regard between us?

5 **Balance:** Do I feel a balance in our relationship? Do we both initiate contact with one another? Are we are both contributing to the success of the project or relationship?

6 **Acceptance:** Do I feel acceptance and ongoing learning in our interaction? Do we look at how we can continuously improve our process of interaction? Do we discuss and dimension unfulfilled expectations? Do we pay attention to the past as helpful information in going forward?

7 **Partnership:** Do I feel partnership in the relationship? Do we share information with each other that impacts our partnership?

Do you see anything missing from this compilation? Please add your thoughts. The important element here is to constantly look at what might be needed to strengthen and continuously improve the relationship. Ask yourself what element might be missing that interferres with relationship success.

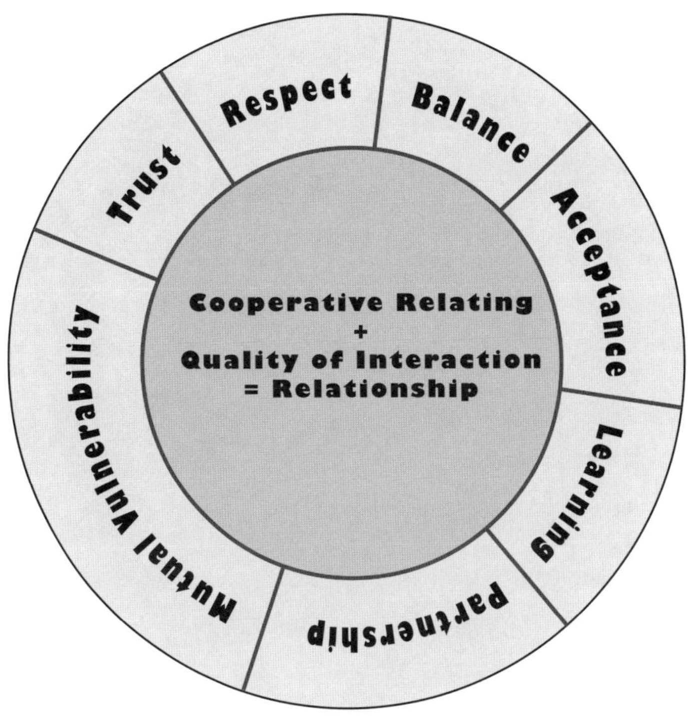

As you reflect on this strategy, what action steps will you immediately take? Add these steps to your calendar right now.

Chapter 22

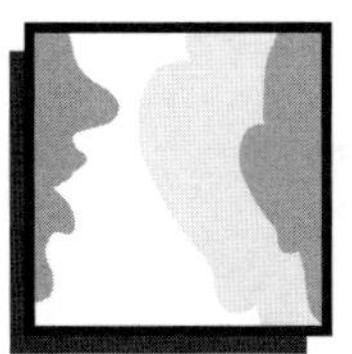

Strategy Four

Listen Three Times as Much With Purpose: *Finding Joint Rhythm & Harmony*

Finding joint rhythm and harmony requires practice, practice, practice AND the ability to adjust your communication style to the needs of your partner and to the situation. When you listen with purpose you are better able to get to the "heart" of an issue, and make relational changes to get back on the same page. Listening three times as much provides the following opportunities. You get more from the interaction, you affirm the person or persons you are listening to, your understanding of the message is greatly enhanced, and you lay the foundation for increased cooperation and collaboration. Following is an assessment to help shed light on your listening awareness.

Respond to the following statements, and rate yourself below. Give yourself 3 points for always; 2 points for sometimes; 1 point for rarely; and 0 points for never.

1. I am aware that to listen effectively I must listen with a purpose. ____

2. I have trained myself to listen three times as much as I speak. ____

3. I listen for understanding rather than evaluation. ____

4. I use clarification to ensure that I am understanding what is being said as the person speaks. ____

5 I recognize the importance of my non-verbal expressions communicated to the speaker. ____

6 I am aware of the word, phrases, or behaviors that will likely make me feel defensive. ____

7 I wait until the speaker has finished before responding. ____

8 People often thank me for listening. ____

9 I concentrate on what the speaker is saying even though other things may distract me. ____

10 I am able to exercise emotional control when listening, even if I disagree with the message. ____

11 I realize that listening purposefully may be the key to understanding. ____

12 I listen for ideas and feelings as well as facts.

Total ________

Score

16 or less → We suggest that you practice, practice, practice.

17-22 → Spend more time on purposeful listening.

23-29 → Purposeful listening is natural for you.

30 + → You are an exceptional listener!

Workshops and books will heighten your awareness. Ongoing attention will help you put into practice this challenging skill.

Following are some guidelines to help you look at your language and guide you toward listening with purpose. Avoid reactive language and absolute terms i.e. "always," and "never."

Reactive Language	Proactive Language
They won't allow for that kind of action.	I'd like to hear more about your ideas on this.
You committed to this project. We're too far down the pike to turn back now.	I'd sure like to keep working together. Are there other ways we could approach this project to increase your satisfaction?
The deadlines are set in stone.	I'm open to revisiting the deadlines to ensure a more quality product while still attending to meeting the urgency needs. What are your thoughts?

Where is conflict in your current relationship? Remember conflict is a natural product of all relationships. It is how you respond that helps keep the relationship functional rather than dysfunctional. How might reframing your responses in proactive language help the partnership? Think about a situation that needs to be addressed. Practice framing your language on the following page.

Reactive Language	Proactive Language

Listening three times as much and using proactive language will also provide a "model" for the other to follow. You will then be able to reframe your frustration into a request.

Example

Frustration expressed in reactive language: You are behind in meeting the deadlines that we agreed upon.

Request expressed in proactive language: I understand you are unable to get back to me on the report as you originally anticipated. I would like to meet the deadline I promised my client; what can I do to help you meet the original time frame?

Remember the tone you use is critical. Communication experts say 93% of what we communicate is nonverbal. Using a collaborative and respectful tone and body language will help you express difficult thoughts and feelings.

What are the action steps that will lead your listening forward? For example, sign up for a course on listening. Or, choose a relationship that needs "listening attention" and practice! Whatever your action is, remember to note it in your calendar!

What action steps will you take?
Add these steps to your calendar right now.

____

____

____

____

____

Strategy Five
Provide a Joyful Experience to Others:
Taking Relationships to the Next Level

As you develop your relationship wisdom, you will be more and more aware of what a joyful experience for the other might be. The essence of this strategy is that there are many ways to provide joyful experiences. Bringing creativity and a fresh approach to all your interactions incorporates joy and escalates your relationships to the next level. The following worksheet helps you capture what you "know" about a person and helps you think through how you might provide a joyful experience for them. Often you may see what needs to be done in the moment. Other times, keeping a journal of all the people you meet and feel a connection to, jotting down their interests, an idea may come that you can later act upon.

	Name	Position	Interests	Ideas
EXAMPLE	Joe Black	Attorney	Adjunct Professor	Provide information concerning teaching

Linking the interest of the other person to the action that we take provides a mutually rewarding joyful experience.

Other helpful hints and reminders in providing joyful experiences to others:

1. Say goodbye to people you meet for the first time.
2. Listen intensely to others.
3. Get out of the way---and allow the person you are speaking with to be the most important person in the room.

What action steps will you immediately take? Add these steps to your calendar right now.

Strategy Six
Consistently Doing the Little Things: *Make The Big Difference*

This strategy emphasizes the power of small acts and how through consistently doing the little things, we make a big difference in the lives of countless others--and who knows, perhaps the world! We are always in relationship to our environment. Our environment includes our families, our friends, our neighbors, our community, our business colleagues, a spiritual force, and nature itself. What are the little things that we do that are relational? If we are hiking in a park, perhaps we pick up litter along the trail. Understanding that we are always in relationship with some one or some aspect of our environment, helps keep us mindful of NetBeing as a way of life. Following are relationship actions that, while not being inclusive, support consistently doing the little things.

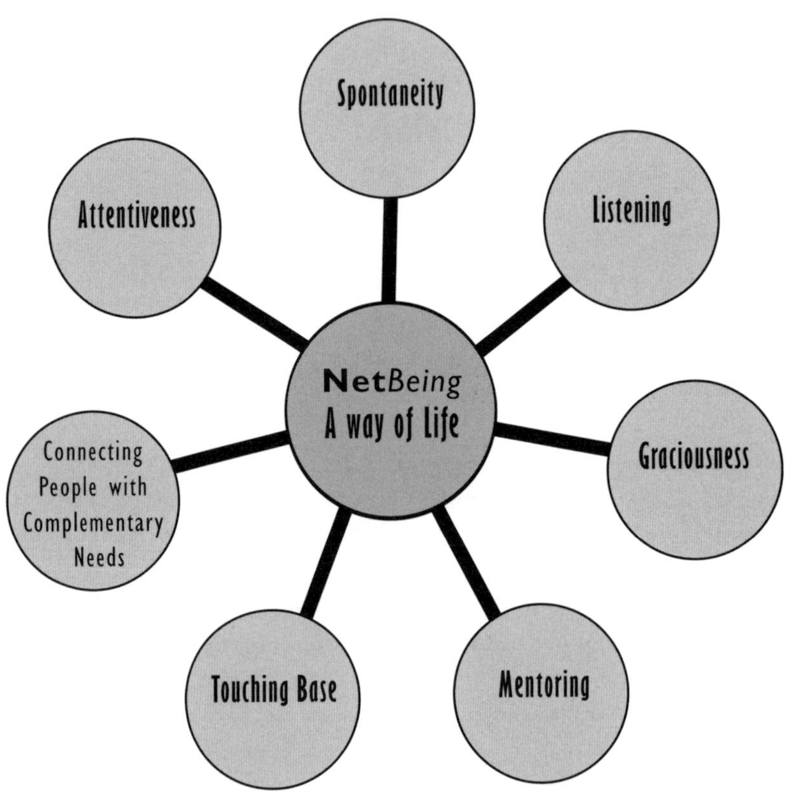
Spontaneity
Attentiveness
Listening
NetBeing
A way of Life
Connecting People with Complementary Needs
Graciousness
Touching Base
Mentoring

Use the following diagram to identify your relationship actions that support you in doing the little things that make a big difference.

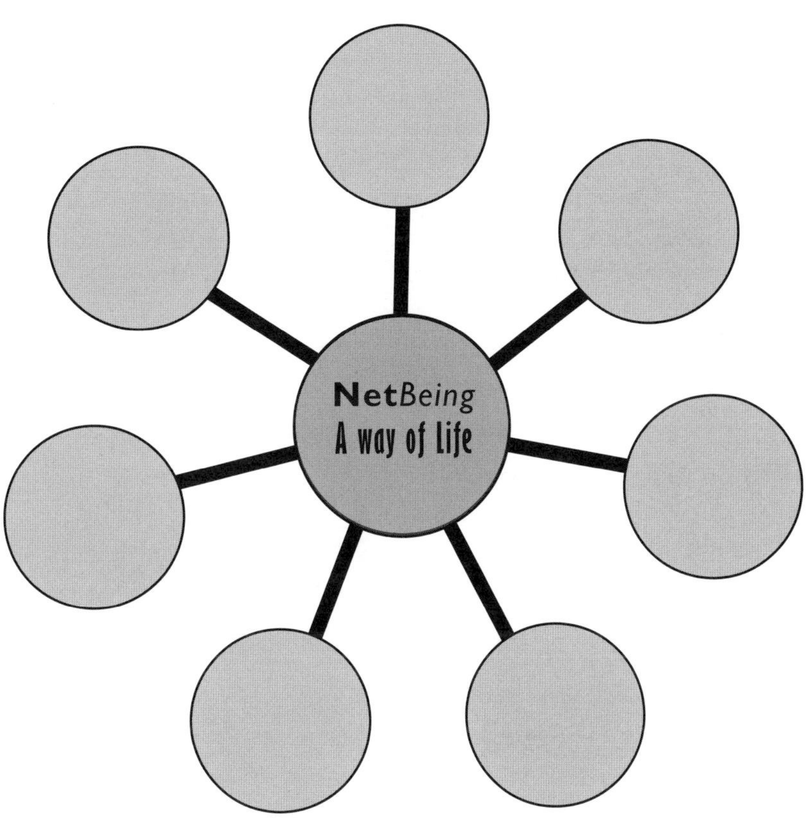

What action steps will you take?
Add these steps to your calendar right now.

Strategy Seven
Create Unparalleled Visibility:
Learning to be Seen & Heard

Increasing visibility increases your ability to be seen and heard. Multiple ways to increase visibility have been presented. By focusing on meeting people who align with your interests, accelerate the possibility for business and personal success. In Part Two, we provided multiple ways that you can create visibility. On the following page you will find a form to help you establish goals to increase your visibility.

Additional examples to increase your visibility include becoming a published writer for local newspapers, doing radio interviews, and releasing excerpts from your newsletter.

A Three Step Process

Think of this as a three step process. First, identify what you are currently doing. Second, think about additional opportunities for meeting people. Third, make a decision and start a process to do it.

What action steps will you take?
Add these steps to your calendar right now.

	Associations	Industry Specific Events	Seminars/ Workshops	Marketing	Athletics/ Hobbies
EXAMPLES	Business Women Connect	Society for H. R. Management	Facilitator Enhancement	Business Cards, Brochure	Racquetball

Chapter 23

Strategy Eight

Make the Connection:

Connecting the Dots

In Strategy One, you identified your intentions for your life. With attention, you go into the world and engage with others. As you engage with others, some individuals stand out more than others as people you would like to know further. You may not know "why" but you sense that they connect to one of your intentions.

I recently met Stacia Matthews. Indianapolis TV personality, she was part of a team of women who spoke at a conference called "Finding Your Voice." Twenty chairs circled around the intimate setting she created. Her first words, softly stated, were, "I don't have a presentation for you....I have a story." We all leaned in! I was immediately hooked. Her story was engaging and I was among several people, who waited to meet her personally after her talk. We exchanged business cards, and I went away with the awareness that she is someone I would like to know further. One of my intentions is continued personal spiritual growth and attention to spirituality in the workplace. She seems to align with that intention.

That's where this strategy takes hold....with awareness. With awareness, I hopefully will recognize the invitation that is appropriate for the next step. From there, I initiate by extending the invitation. Her response will set the tone for additional contact, and may determine if mutuality exists.

Following is a chart to help you heighten your awareness of the various relationships that surround you. Many of these individuals may clearly "make sense" on your path to your intention. Many that you record here may be based solely on a "feeling" that there is something you are to do or learn together. As you meet people, collect their business cards, or jot down their name on a napkin. It may also be helpful to use a worksheet such as this designed to capture the "feeling" associated with the person. Make up a chart for each of your intentions. While many of them overlap, this is one way to ensure that these individuals stay in your consciousness.

Examples

Name	Sensation	Awareness	Tangible Information	Question	Initiate
Stacia Matthews	Spiritual Depth; Approachable; Helps others through her story.	I'd like to know her;	Walker;Health bytes newsper-sonality	How?Business? Personal	Invite to discussion group; invite to speak

Worksheets such as this will help you better "track" the relationships that engage you, and align with your life intentions. Use this worksheet as a reminder to connect the dots when idea meets up with energy attraction....or where the past meets up with the present.

A "Make the Connection" Tip

Before going into a family celebration, a large business conference, or a NetBeing event:

- Think about your intention.
- Who would you like to connect with?
- What conversation or deeper connection would you like to have?
- Focus on building a bridge to another.
- What "feeling" would you like to foster?
- What would you like to take away?

Now walk into that room, suspending your thinking and trust the flow of synchronicity.

What action steps will you take? Add these steps to your calendar right now.

____

____

____

____

____

Strategy Nine

Travel at the Velocity of a Fast-Paced World: *Flowing at the Speed of Change*

Speed is a driving force. When we're meeting individuals, we are meeting them one at a time and the opportunity to quickly move into a relationship posture is now! Focusing time and attention then is a quickening fueled by possibility, alignment, precision, and clarity as we move forward at the speed of change.

Chapter 23

Here are straight-forward tips to move you more quickly into the flow of a Fast-Paced world:

- **Let people know what you're doing.** They may need your services, or be able to help you, or know someone else who may be interested in what you are offering.

- **Look closely at how you build your relationships now.** Challenge your thinking on what you do, and most importantly how you do it.

- **Measure the time between first meeting someone to when you send out a "nice to meet you" letter.** What is your success when you follow up within 24 hours? What is your success when you follow up within three months?

- **Talk to others about how they do what they do.** This helps you better understand who they are and what is important to them.

- **Develop a broad-base of partnership relationships.** We are referring here to our clients, our suppliers, our associates, and our employees.

- **Don't burn bridges.** Prior business relationships will fuel you toward future business opportunities. Avoid negative story telling about prior relationships. Use previous challenges as "learning" opportunities. In talking about these learning curves, share how you personally learned from those experiences. You will have more credibility and will demonstrate how learning occurs through experience and in relationship.

- **Preparation encounters opportunity.** Using your "whole" self, the fundamental core of NetBeing, be ready to join in when an opportunity that speaks to you presents itself.

- **Be, or NetBe, wherever you are.** Whether you are in France, New Mexico, or New Zealand, you have opportunities to make connections and develop relationships.

- **Look for multiple ways to market and speak about your business.** This information can be found through a marketing firm, industry magazines, or by asking others in your position.

- **Keep infusing your business initiatives with new energy.** Get others excited about what you are doing. Know when to bring in additional help and or marketing.

Building urgency into relationships is a proactive process. Being proactive creates excitement and enthusiasm. And with excitement and enthusiasm comes greater success and opportunities with others.

What action steps will you take?
Add these steps to your calendar right now.

____
____
____
____
____
____

Strategy Ten
Shorten Learning Curves:
Move Into Dream Fulfillment

As you might guess, this book project has provided numerous opportunities for Ron and me to apply each of these strategies. This strategy, shortening learning curves, has proven to be a particular catalyst to fuel us forward.

We realized over lunch after a racquetball game that we both were passionate about relationships and relationship success. Ron's writings about networking and his passion about another level beyond what is happening in the mainstream complemented well with my writings and passion around helping people hold a relationship vision that opens the possibility of co-creation and partnership. Within 30 minutes, we identified an overlapping purpose and this book partnership was launched. Within a year, it is finished. How do two people who do not know each other very well come together and join forces toward this kind of project or any other? We would like to say, from our experience, not just this one but many others, it is through shortening the learning curve. Following are two graphics. One illustrates a long learning curve where side roads are taken as individuals lose track of the project vision.

This is contrasted to a shortened learning curve that focuses on finding common ground. When we focus on common ground and what is most important in a given moment, we keep the bigger picture of our purpose and intentions before us. We work straight ahead, using direct communication and staying mindful of the context. Trusting that the other has our best interest in mind, we move ahead at a pace fueled with positive energy. See if you can picture this for yourself.

Long Learning Curve

Short Learning Curve:

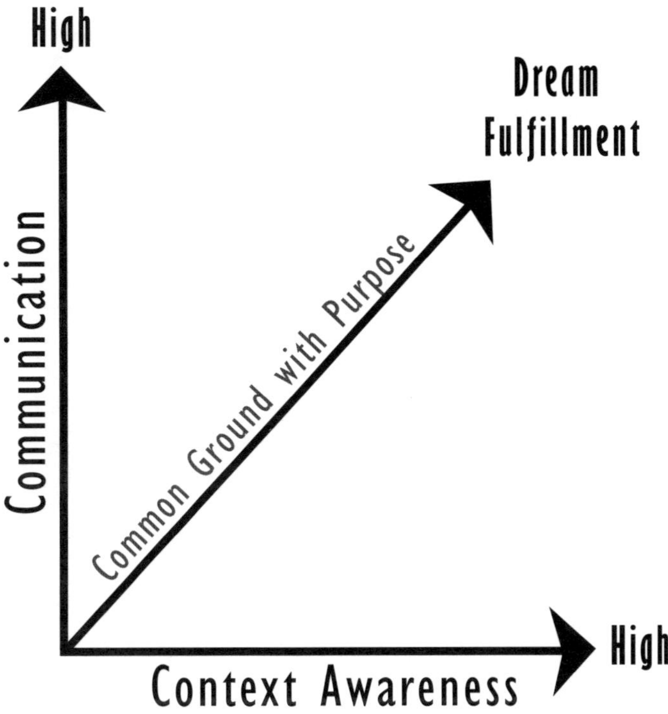

To help shorten the learning curve, there may be issues you are facing. Following are questions for your consideration. Think about one of your personal or business partners. Respond to the following questions:

1. What project emerged between the two of you?
2. What problems, issues, needs or opportunities can the two of you respond to and address together?
3. What resources, information, time frame will support your project?
4. Who will be impacted by this project, and how will they be affected? How might they be involved in the project?
5. How will you know if you are individually and jointly successful?

6. What adjustments need to be made as you move forward toward project completion (dream fulfillment)?

7. How do your channels of communication support your project and shorten the learning curve? (i.e. email, voice mail, direct communication, talking about prior experiences or learning curves.)

8. Are you looking out for each other as well as your joint interests throughout this process? If not, what improvements need to be made?

9. What challenges are you currently facing: financial, communication, resources, etc.?

10. What steps taken together would move you more expediently and more closely to project completion?

Scenario Planning

There are times for extensive market studies and long term plans. During those times, by all means incorporate a longer approach to moving toward a joint collaborative effort.

Scenario planning will help you move much more quickly and may be just what you need for the joint project at hand. Write a brief case study with the objective and with as many variables that you can think of. Balance your optimistic thoughts with opposite possibilities to make sure that you are encompassing all possible contingencies. Include as much of the "unpredictable" as possible. Include what can go right, and what can go wrong. Then discuss the scenario and how you might deal with challenges that might arise.

What action steps will you take?
Add these steps to your calendar right now.

Chapter 24

Strategy Eleven

Moving Into Legendary Status:

Going From the Ordinary to the Extraordinary

A consistent focus in moving from the ordinary to the extraordinary moves us to legendary status. Rethinking what we do, looking for ways to become more resourceful, and having a process and project management focus will help establish this exceptional foundation. Going from the ordinary to the extraordinary calls for continual self reflection of how you are performing in relationship. Self Reflection provides information to help you improve your efforts and move **you** toward extraordinary relationship satisfaction.

Here is a simple process to help you reflect back.

From Ordinary to Extraordinary

Imagine looking at your life through a movie projector. Slow the projector down and stop on those moments that were exceptional.

Focus in on one and then answer the following:

1. Describe the experience.

___

___

___

2. What was it about the experience that separated it from all the rest?

___

___

___

3 What made it so extraordinary?

4 How did it feel?

Perhaps you focused your mind's eye on a holiday, a trip to the beach, a successful project, your honeymoon, the first day on a new job, or your first kiss. Whatever it was, the experience came with an extraordinary feeling, and probably came in relationship with at least one other person. How can you help your partners achieve this feeling? Ask good questions! Ask what makes the difference between good or great for your partner. By asking good questions and purposeful listening, you'll gain insight from verbal and nonverbal cues, and information derived from reading between the lines.

A Project Management Focus

A project begins in relationship with at least one other person, or one element of your environment. There are many considerations as you examine all the elements toward the extraordinary completion of a project. The following modified version of the fishbone diagram created by Karoru Ishikawa provides food for thought to help you think about the aspects to consider in moving a project forward.

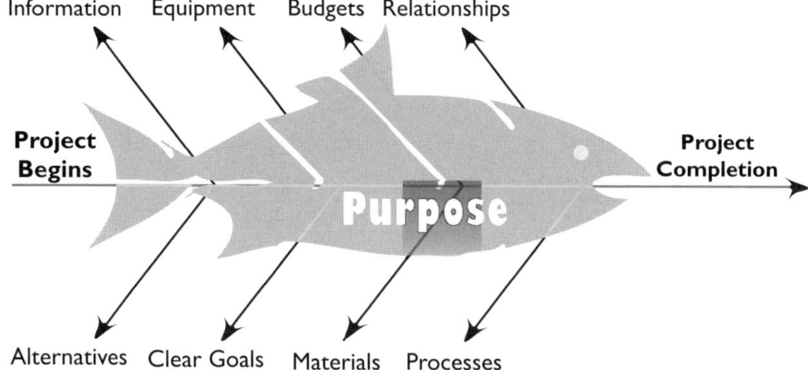

What is the vision that both of you have for the project? What resources do you need to move your project, and therefore your relationship, toward legendary status? Use the fishbone outline below to diagram that for yourself.

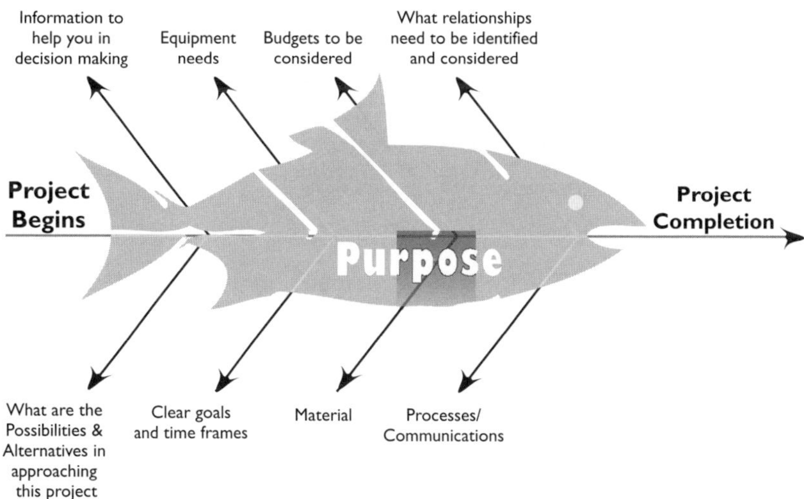

Project management is a matter of identifying all the important factors, and then creating a system to move your project and your relationship forward. A project management focus provides a framework and makes it possible to move from the ordinary to the extraordinary.

What action steps will you take?
Add these steps to your calendar right now.

____

____

____

____

____

Strategy Twelve

Become Technologically Savvy: *Building the Techno Advantage*

Thanks to the Internet, and the latest innovations in technology, the confines of time and space have disappeared. Communication technology will help you better meet the increased expectations for the ever changing market. Strengthen your personal and business relationships by diagnosing the best channel for the specific relationship in mind.

Level the Playing Field With Technology

Communicating electronically is immediate, cost-effective, efficient, and 100% documentable. It is a matter of plugging in with the equipment that is "right" for you.

Scan the following technology publications and sites as you develop your technological advantage.

Technology Publications & Websites

- **Technology review www.technologyreview.com**
  Since 1899, Technology Review has been MIT's magazine of innovation. Their mission statement is, "to promote the under standing of emerging technologies and their impact on business and society."

- **Educational Technology reports from the Dept. of Education** www.ed.gov/Technology/reports.html

- **PC magazine www.pcmag.com**
  PC Magazine is an important technology publication that delivers authoritative, labs-based comparative reviews of com puting and Internet products. The PC Magazine defines technology for e-business and provides in-depth reviews and accurate, repeatable testing from PC Magazine Labs placed in the unique context of today's business technology landscape.

- **Computer World www.computerworld.com**
  Unlike any other IT information source, Computerworld has a proud heritage that speaks volumes about continuous change, adaptation and brand loyalty. Thirty-five years since launching as "the newsweekly for the computer community", Computerworld remains at the forefront of IT Leaders' information needs.

- **Info World www.infoworld.com**
  InfoWorld Media Group delivers in-depth coverage and evaluation of IT products for technology experts involved in major purchase decisions for their companies. InfoWorld reaches readers through its integrated online, print, events, and research channels.

  InfoWorld provides specialized IT coverage for the CTO, senior-most company executives who are deeply steeped in technology expertise and experience.

- **IDG www.idg.net**
  IDG's Technology Directory serves the needs of global technology decision-makers by providing immediate access to trusted technology news, information and resources from around the world. Peruse technology content through our state of the art search, by category, or find the latest breaking information directly on our home page.

- **Darwin www.darwinmag.com**
  For senior executives intent on successfully navigating through technology change, Darwin offers the latest tools and insight.

- **CIO Magazine www.cio.com**
  CIO Magazine is an award winning publication, serving the needs of CIOs and other senior information technology experts since 1987.

- **Information week www.informationweek.com**
  InformationWeek is a weekly print magazine that reaches 440,000 business and IT professionals at more than a quarter million businesses. It's read by CIOs, IT managers, business managers, and information technology professionals among others. The magazine provides in-depth analysis, news, research and perspectives on the latest business technology trends.

  While there are many other publications for your review, starting with some of these will certainly support your understanding and working knowledge of what's available.

The Internet: Trade Show Listings

Visit trade shows. While there are many local technology programs that are put on by your local Chamber, the following national programs are also available

- **The Trade Show Plaza www.tradeshowplaza.com**
  The Premier resource center for: Trade Shows, Technology Conferences, Forums, Computer Expos, Web Seminars and Tech Events Worldwide.

- **IT Service Management Forum**
  www.internettradeshowlist.com
  List is a complete guide of Internet conferences and technology trade shows & seminars including a trade show directory with descriptions, schedules.

- **Information Technology Exposition and Conference**
  www.goitec.com
  ITEC builds a strong foundation for lasting relationships between technology solutions providers and IT decision makers. ITEC is by far the nation's leading series of regional information technology events.

Website Design

While you can craft your own professional site with off-the-shelf software, local internet service providers (ISP) are great partners to help you establish quality site design and web site hosting inexpensively. Finding these partners is also at your fingertips. Go to:

- **www.thelist.com:** Here you will find a comprehensive directory of ISPs. You can narrow your search by state or area code. You will find information about rates, contact information, and specific services.

- **www.internic.net:** This is the registration clearing house for domain names, or the part of a URL that falls between the www. And the .com or .net. Registration costs are minimal-although, domain names can become quite valuable!

Continuing to develop your technological savvy will truly help you level the playing field today and in the future.

What action steps will you take?
Add these steps to your calendar right now.

Strategy Thirteen

Become a Global Partner:

One World, One Playing Field

This vast playing field is exciting and has great potential. This strategy has stressed the critical importance of looking at these endeavors intellectually, and securing professional and legal advice along the way. As you develop your global expertise, the questions you ask as you go forward are vitally important. Talking to others who have developed global partnerships will also help you learn through their hard earned lessons.

To help you establish a plan of action, two sets of guidelines are provided.

The first set is to help you raise questions wherever your partner lives. The second set is geared more toward developing partnerships with individuals in other countries.

- **Financial strength:** How financially viable is your potential partner? How long have they been in business? Are you aware of their reputation in the global community? How important is it to know their net worth, and/or financial situation?

- **Business strategy:** Is your potential partners' business strategy similar or complementary to yours? Do they have partnerships with other companies? What markets do they serve?

- **Are they an innovator?** What type of leadership in the marketplace does this person exemplify?

- **Quality leadership:** What examples and how do business references support a quality focus?

- **Top management strength:** What management skills or teams do they have in place to support the project?

- **Product/ Service reliability:** What is the reputation of their products or services?

In addition, when considering a global marketplace, it is important to consider social, cultural, economic, demographic, lifestyle, technological and other environmental factors. It is important to recognize that each country has different legal and value systems. The following is a list of considerations. We urge you to research these aspects as you continue to develop global partnerships.

- Cultural and ideological differences

- Foreign laws, bureaucracy, and governments

- International monetary factors
- Political instability
- Economic viability
- Privacy issues
- Language barriers

As with any business function, a well-defined strategy and organized plan of action can be the difference between success and failure. Relationships across the globe are no different.

Look to the following for information to help you deepen your understanding of the global marketplace:

- **http://www.wtamu.edu/~sanwar.bus/otherlinks.htm**

  Offers links to information to global companies, markets and industries in addition to links to international intellectual capital and knowledge management plus useful websites and search engines. (Or email: sanwar@mail.wtamu.edu)

- **www.mindexchange.com/international-hr.htm**

  The international employment & hr directory is a source of information and services for expatriates and international business executives.

What action steps will you take?
Add these steps to your calendar right now.

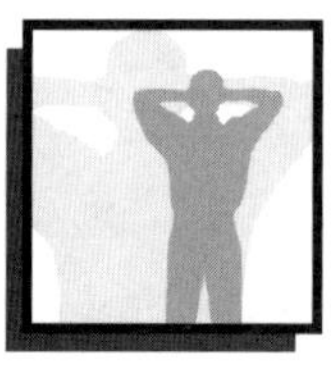

Strategy Fourteen

Look Back to Move Forward:
Taking the Moment & Dancing With It

Taking the moment and dancing with it is truly an art. By going back in time and rediscovering connections from the past, you're doing just that. Look up someone from your past, and "notice" if there is a shift possible for a new relationship to emerge.

Here's how to go about finding some of those individuals you wish to connect with.

Listed below are a few websites to aid you in your search:

- **www.WhoWhere.com**
  The leading communications guide enabling people and businesses worldwide to find, connect and collaborate witH each other by providing directories of email.
- **www.AnyWho.com**
  Use AnyWho to find: phone numbers, addresses, maps & directions for Business and People in the US.
- **www.whitepages.com**
  Find a person with either first name, last name, city or zip code.
- **www.reunitetonight.com**
  This website advertises the largest database of phone and address records.

Keep in mind that some of these companies may charge you to provide the information you are requesting. There is no cost for you to just type in the name of the person you are looking for. Don't be surprised if the person just happens to pop up in any of the popular search engines on the Internet. This typically works really well when the person you are looking for has gained some kind of visibility in their current profession, i.e. a historical person, a singer, or a published author.

Results are available instantly.

With that said, go for it. Search out as many individuals from your past with whom you want to reconnect. Begin the process of rebuilding those incredible relationships you loved from the past; the process of taking yesteryear's relationships and bringing them into the present. In essence, you're continuing on the path of NetBeing!

Good Luck, and keep us informed about how this works for you.

What action steps will you take?
Add these steps to your calendar right now.

Chapter 25

Strategy Fifteen

Continuous Development With Purpose: *Ongoing Enhancement of Life Through Personal & Professional Growth*

Jane: This entire strategy provides a process for you to tap into your greater vitality and intelligence by determining your purpose, developing your ability to discern, and using the four principles of continuous learning found in Part Two.

Applying the paradigm of mastery, we propose individuals pass through three distinct levels as they proceed toward becoming increasingly effective in their life learning process.

Level One: An ever-changing economy and world presents the opportunity for everyone in today's workforce to go back to basics in the development of new skills. As lifelong learners, we are continually moving from novice to expert. As a novice, you have the desire to learn the skill but haven't acquired confidence and competence. You may be confident that you can learn the skills but are unsure how to put these skills into practice. You rely on others to introduce new frameworks and models, you practice new skills in a safe environment, and you seek out mentors and coaches to help you along the way. (If you are dedicated to a lifetime of learning, you are always at the novice stage in certain areas of your life i.e., learning a new language, writing a novel, or learning a leadership practice.)

Level Two: In this stage, learners are taking new skills into their relationships, and through a diagnostic process, practicing these new skills along with others. While you still may feel awkward, you are beginning to feel more confident and at ease. You are beginning to see the many variables in the environment, the total system, and perhaps even the intricacies of the world as a whole. You understand that there is no one size fits all approach.

Level Three: Confidence and competence is high. You use a diagnostic approach and your skills have become second nature. You trust your instincts. You test your skills constantly through one-on-one interactions and group presentations. You measure your success by the overall satisfaction of the relationship. You have identified the "right" questions that help you identify system problems, barriers for mutual success, and the resources that you need to foster a more productive and empowering relationship. You understand competing forces within the environment, work well with others, and have created a learning and continuous improvement environment; you have become an expert in this area.

Remember, within a lifetime of learning, you are constantly moving from level one (novice) to level two, and finally to level three (expert). You may be a novice in one or several areas of your life, and an expert at one or several other areas of your life.

Develop a Learning Process

1. Continuously apply self knowledge and attention to purpose, goals, and objectives.
2. Self evaluate and have others provide observations and recommendations.
3. Identify specific areas for improvement.
4. Identify role models and mentors for areas you wish to develop.
5. Identify courses or workshops to help you develop new competencies.
6. Broaden experiences by taking initiative in meeting new people in new settings.
7. Read books that align with your development (like this one!)
8. Connect with others within and outside of your organization.

9 Review your progress and set new goals as necessary.

10 Solicit dialogue on an ongoing basis in all relationships. Use the dialogue as a springboard for adjusting your strategy.

11 Keep a notebook of feedback, thoughts, accomplishments, behaviors, and insights to help you stay focused and plan forward.

12 Develop a portfolio to capture your process of learning.

The following provides a visual for you to look at your learning and align accordingly. Unlearning is examining that which no longer serves you. What habits, what thinking, what behaviors would you like to unlearn? What technical or non technical skills would align to your goals and objectives. What expert knowledge would help you in your field? What practices, workshops, or courses would help you improve your communication skills?

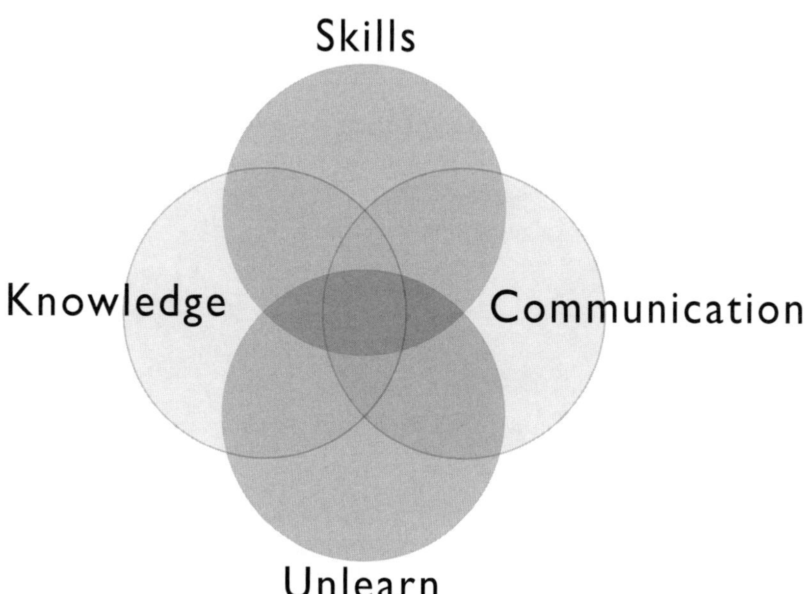

Chapter 25

Application Exercise

What skills fit into each of these columns? In Level One, indicate new skills you would like to learn and are currently focusing on. In Level Two, note skills you are currently working on, and are beginning to feel success. In the third column, note expert skills. Remember, a continuous learning path, calls for an ongoing integration of new skills and competencies, where your portfolio captures a lifetime of learning and expertise.

A Portfolio in Progress

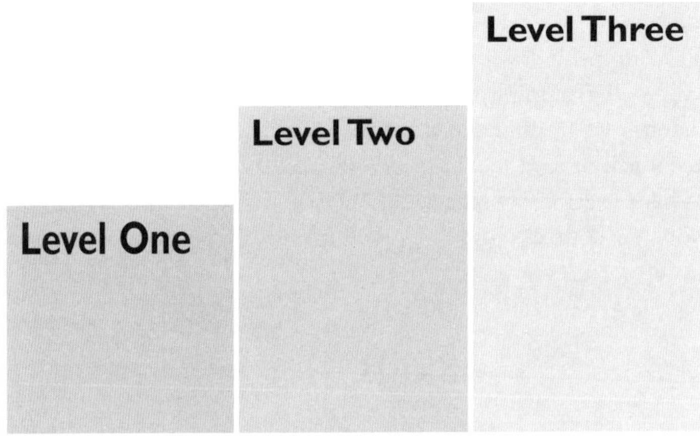

What action steps will you take?
Add these steps to your calendar right now.

Summary of Part Three

You have written out your goals for each strategy, expressed them positively, and committed to making every effort possible to foster the relationships you most desire. We hope that you will keep your plan of action close by, refer to it often, and make adjustments along your unique road to stronger and deeper relationships. Your diagnostic mind, your heart, and your physical being must be actively engaged as you continue along changing this plan as needed. This plan will be like a friend you reach out to when you are faced with the proverbial fork in the road and unsure of the direction to take. As you walk through your life with various relationships, determining what is needed for the particular situation at hand, you will guide yourself to the relationship strategy that will best serve you.

Chapter 26

Final Thoughts

How does one consciously pursue deep change within relationship without drawing attention to that effort as a technique--but because we actually care? That has been our intention throughout the book; that at the core of all strategies is acting out of a deep sense of caring for ourselves, for our personal relationships, for our professional relationships, and for our environment at large.

We believe there is a "new" collaborative energy around business relationships. It is our intent to foster this new kind of business philosophy. We see its emergence being embraced in the many people we've talked to. We hope we have provided guidance to help enhance the process.

Thomas Kuhn, in his book *The Structure of Scientific Revolutions* shows how almost every significant breakthrough in science is first a break with old patterns and with old paradigms of thinking.

In this book, we hope you have challenged your current thinking process. Perhaps you've decided you are already a natural when it comes to developing quality relationships. Perhaps you've added a few new tools for your toolbox...or perhaps you've shifted your way of thinking and developed a new paradigm for moving your personal and professional relationships to the next level, through the process of a relationship mindset. Remember the power is truly in the connection.

Whatever the case, we wish you well and happy trails, and your best life. See you along the way.

Jane George-Surges and Ron Sukenick

APPENDIX

Associations

Trade and professional associations offer a wealth of networking and relationship building opportunities. To encourage you to make the most from this valuable resource, we have listed over 130 associations.

There are thousands of associations throughout the country and the world where people come together on a monthly basis in order to share ideas, information and their resources.

Our listing provides a good starting point covering in excess of 40 classifications and listing the most significant and well known associations within each field.

To be really thorough, we suggest that you visit your local library or web search, and research the association directories specifically of interest to you.

You can consult the American Society of Associations on the web at www.asaenet.org

Accounting

American Women's Society of Certified Public Accountants
http://www.awscpa.org
The American Woman's Society of Certified Public Accountants (AWSCPA) purpose is to help members achieve their full potential and to actively promote equity within the profession.
136 South Keowee Street, Dayton, OH 45402, Tel: 937-222-1872 / 800-AWSCPA-1, Fax: 937-222-5794, Email: info@awscpa.org

American Accounting Association
http://www.aaahq.org
The American Accounting Association promotes worldwide excellence in

accounting education, research and practice.
5717 Bessie Drive, Sarasota, FL 34233-2399, USA, Tel: 941-921-7747 - Fax: 941-923-4093, Email: Office@aaahq.org

American Institute of Certified Public Accountants

http://www.aicpa.org/

The American Institute of Certified Public Accountants is the national, professional organization for all Certified Public Accountants. Its mission is to provide members with the resources, information, and leadership that enable them to provide valuable services in the highest professional manner to benefit the public as well as employers and clients.
1211 Avenue of the Americas, New York, NY 10036-8775, USA, Tel: 212-596-6200, Fax: 212-596-6213

American Society of Women Accountants

http://www.aswa.org

ASWA was formed in 1938 to increase the opportunities for women in all fields of accounting and finance. The first chapter was chartered in Indianapolis, Indiana. Members include partners in national, regional and local CPA firms, financial officers, controllers, academicians, financial analysts and data processing consultants, recent college graduates and women returning to the work force. The majority of its members have attained professional certifications such as CPA, CMA, CIA, and CFP. The mission of ASWA is to enable women in all accounting and related fields to achieve their full personal, professional and economic potential and to contribute to the future development of their profession. 1255 Lynnfield Rd. #257 Memphis, TN 38119 Tel: 901-680-0470

National Society of Accountants

http://www.nsacct.org/

NSA and its affiliates represent more than 30,000 independent practitioners who provide accounting, tax, auditing, financial and estate planning to 19 million individuals and businesses. For more than 50 years, NSA has supported its members with resources and representation to protect their right to practice, build credibility and grow the profession.
1010 N. Fairfax St., Alexandria, VA. 22314, USA, Tel: 800-966-6679 / 703-549-6400, Fax: 703-549-2984, Email: members@nsacct.org

Administrative Professionals

The International Association of Administrative Professionals
http://www.iaap-hq.com
The International Association of Administrative Professionals (IAAP) is a not-for-profit professional association with 40,000 members and affiliates and 600+ chapters worldwide. The association works in partnership with employers to promote excellence. Its members include administrative assistants, executive secretaries, office coordinators, information specialists, and related administrative professionals. Many corporations, educational institutions, students, and international affiliate organizations also belong to IAAP:
10502 NW Ambassador Drive, PO Box 20404, Kansas City, MO 64195-0404, USA, Tel: 816-891-6600, Fax: 816-891-9118, Email: service@iaap-hq.org

Advertising

American Advertising Federation
www.aaf.org
As the "Unifying Voice for Advertising," the American Advertising Federation (AAF), headquartered in Washington, D.C., with a Western Region office in Newport Beach, Calif., is the trade association that represents 50,000 professionals in the advertising industry. AAF's 130 corporate members are advertisers, agencies and media companies that comprise the nation's leading brands and corporations. AAF has a national network of 210 ad clubs and connects the industry with an academic base through its 210 college chapters.
1101 Vermont Ave, #500 Washington, DC 20005, Tel: 202-898-0089

International Advertising Association
www.iaaglobal.org
342 Madison Ave # 2000 New York, NY 10017, Tel: 212-682-2500
The International Advertising Association is a one-of-a-kind strategic partnership which champions the common interests of all the disciplines across the full spectrum of marketing communications - from advertisers to media companies to agencies to direct marketing firms - as well as individual practitioners.

Banking

American Bankers Association
http://www.aba.com/
The American Bankers Association (ABA) is the only national trade and professional association that encompasses the entire banking community, from small community banks to large bank holding companies. ABA members represent approximately 90% of the commercial banking industry's total assets, and about 94% of ABA members are community banks with assets less than $500 million.
1120 Connecticut Avenue N.W., Washington, DC 20036, Tel: 800-BANKERS

Mortgage Bankers Association of America
www.mbaa.org
The Mortgage Bankers Association seeks to create an environment that enables its members to invest in communities and achieve their business objectives. The association creates this environment by developing innovative business tools, educating and training industry professionals, providing a gathering place for the sharing of ideas, acting as the industry's voice on legislative and regulatory issues, and developing open and fair standards and practices for the industry.
1125 15th St. NW Washington, DC 20005, Tel: 205-861-6500

Better Business Bureau

The Council of Better Business Bureaus
http://www.bbb.org/
The Council of Better Business Bureaus is committed to promoting and fostering the highest ethical relationship between businesses and the public through voluntary self-regulation, consumer and business education, and service excellence.
4200 Wilson Blvd Suite 800, Arlington, VA 22203-1838, Tel : 703-276-0100, Fax : 703-525-8277

Broadcasting

The National Association of Broadcasters
http://www.nab.org
A full-service trade association which represents the interests of free, over-

the-air radio and television broadcasters.
1771 N Street NW, Washington, DC 20036, Tel: 202-429-5300, Fax: 202-429-4199, Email: nab@nab.org

Business Networking

Business Networks International
http://www.bni.com
BNI is an 18 year old business and professional organization that allows only one person from each trade or profession to join a chapter. With over 3,022 active chapters, and 63,000 members, it is the most successful business referral organization in the world.
199 South Monte Vista Avenue Suite 6, San Dimas, CA 91773, Tel: 800-825-8286 / 909-305-1818, Fax: 909-305-1811

Leads Clubs, Inc
www.leadsclub.com
Founded in 1978, Leads Club is the oldest networking organization in the world. Leads Club is open to business owners, professionals, sales people and managers seeking to begin or expand a business.
PO Box 279 Carlsbad, CA 92018, (800) 783-3761

LeTip International
LeTip.com
LeTip is a professional organization of men and women dedicated to the highest standards of competence and service. It's primary purpose is to give and receive qualified business tips or leads. Members will, at all times, maintain the highest professional integrity. Each business category is represented by one member and conflicts of interest are disallowed.
LeTip International, Inc. P.O. Box 178130 San Diego, CA 92177-9926 Tel: (800) 25-LETIP (53847)

Networking For Professionals
http://www.networkingfor professionals.com
Networking For Professionals' mission is to bring together motivated professionals exclusively for the purpose of business networking. Networking For Professionals was started by its founders to provide a powerful alternative to traditional networking so that new business contacts could be quickly facilitated. Networking for Professionals began in New York in the spring of 2002 and has been rapidly growing ever since. Though most of

its members are still based in New York and the Tri-State region, membership is on the rise in other states and internationally.
Tel: 718-625-1369, Email: membership@NetworkingForProfessionals.com

Professional Referral Exchange
www.prorefx.com
PRE is a networking organization that helps professionals build business through the exchange of qualified business referrals. PRE has Chapters across the United States and has spent years developing effective systems for both licensee's and members. Tel: 800-929-LEAD.

Chamber of Commerce

United States Chamber of Commerce
http:uschamber.com
Whether it's lobbying the Federal Government, fighting in the courts, or offering special member benefits and discounts, the U.S. Chamber is working for you.
1615 H Street NW, Washington, DC 20062-2000, Tel: 202-659-6000, Email: custsvc@uschamber.com

International Chamber of Commerce
http://www.chamber-of -commerce.com
ICC is the world business organization, the only representative body that speaks with authority on behalf of enterprises from all sectors in every part of the world. ICC promotes an open international trade and investment system and the market economy. Its conviction that trade is a powerful force for peace and prosperity dates from the organization's origins early in the last century. The small group of far-sighted business leaders who founded ICC called themselves "the merchants of peace".
William Stibravy, ICC Permanent Representative, c/o US Council for International Business, 1212, Avenue of the Americas, New York, NY 10036, Tel: 212-354-4480, Fax: 212-575-0327, Email: wstibravy@uscib.org
International Chamber of Commerce, 38 Cours Albert 1er, 75008 Paris, France, Tel:.33-1-49-53-28-28, Fax: 33-1-49-53-28-59, Email: webmaster@iccwbo.org

Computing and Information Sciences

American Library Association
www.ala.org
Its mission is "to provide leadership for the development, promotion, and improvement of library and information services and the profession of librarianship in order to enhance learning and ensure access to information for all."

50 East Huron St. Chicago, IL 60611, Tel: 312-944-6780

American Society for Information Science and Technology
http://asis.org/
Since 1937, the American Society for Information Science and Technology (ASIS&T) has been the society for information professionals leading the search for new and better theories, techniques, and technologies to improve access to information.
ASIS&T brings together diverse streams of knowledge, focusing what might be disparate approaches into novel solutions to common problems. ASIS&T bridges the gaps not only between disciplines but also between the research that drives and the practices that sustain new developments.
8720 Georgia Ave. # 501 Silver Springs, MD 20910, Tel: 301-495-0900

Independent Computer Consultants Association
www.icca.org
ICCA is a national not-for-profit association based in St. Louis that provides professional development opportunities and business support programs for independent computer consultants. ICCA has chapters in many major metropolitan areas representing nearly 1250 consulting firms nationwide. ICCA is one of twelve major computer-related associations represented as an Affiliate of the Institute of Certified Computer Professionals.

1131 S. Towne Square, # F St. Louis, MO 63123, Tel: 314-892-1675

Consulting

Association of Independent Consultants
http://www.aiconsult.ca/
The Association of Independent Consultants (AIC) helps you find special-

ists, experts and outsourced contractors in many fields.
15 Wilson Street, Markham, Ontario Canada L3P 1M9, Tel: 416-410-8163, Fax: 905-294-9435, Email: info@aiconsult.ca

Professional and Technical Consultants Association
www.patca.org/patca
Professional and Technical Consultants Association (PATCA) is a non-profit professional association of independent consultants and principals in small consulting firms. PATCA was founded in 1975, with the objective of being recognized as the best source for direct access to a network of the best professional and technical consultants. PATCA takes pride in the high caliber of our members. Our members offer services in a wide range of consulting fields, including hardware and software engineering, marketing, management, human resources, and many other technical and non-technical fields. The membership process includes verification of professional consulting references.
P.O. Box 4143 Mountain View, CA 94040, Tel: 415-903-8305

Credit Management

National Association of Credit Management
http://www.nacm.org
The NACM represents more than 34,000 business-credit grantors in manufacturing, wholesaling, service industries, and financial institutions. NACM was founded in 1896 to promote good laws for sound credit, protect businesses against fraudulent debtors, improve the interchange of credit information, develop better credit practices and methods, and establish a code of ethics.
8840 Columbia 100 Parkway, Columbia, Maryland 21045, Tel: 410-740-5560, Fax: 410 - 740-5574, Email: info@nacm.org

Customer Service

The International Customer Service Association
http://www.icsa.com
International Customer Service Association (ICSA) promotes the development and awareness of the customer service profession.
401 North Michigan Avenue, Chicago, IL 60611, Tel: 800-360-4272 / 312-321-6800, Email: icsa@sba.com

Design

American Society of Interior Designers

www.asid.org

The American Society of Interior Designers (ASID) is a nonprofit professional society representing the interests of interior designers and the interior design community.

ASID is the leading professional organization for interior designers with the largest residential and commercial membership. With more than 34,500 members, ASID establishes a common identity for professionals and businesses in the field of interior design. 608 Massachusetts Ave. NE Washington, DC 20002, Tel: 202-546-3480

Industrial Designers Society of America

www.idsa.org

IDSA is the voice of the industrial design profession, advancing the quality and positive impact of design.

1142 E. Walker Road Great Falls, VA 22066, Tel: 703-759-0100

Economics

American Economic Association

http://www.vanderbilt.edu/AEA/

The American Economic Association (AEA), organized in 1885 and incorporated in 1923, represents approximately 22,000 economists and 5,500 institutes.

2014 Broadway Suite 305, Nashville, TN 37203, Tel: 615-322-2595, Fax: 615-343-7590

Executives

American Society of Association Executives

http://www/asaenet.org

Since 1920 the American Society of Association Executives (ASAE) has provided members with the resources they need to enhance performance and ensure continued growth and success. With more than 23,000 members worldwide, ASAE is the leading organization in the field of association management.

1575 I St. N.W., Washington, DC 20005-1103, Tel: 202-626-2723, Fax: 202-371-8825, Email: partnerships@asaenet.org

International Executives Association

http://www.ieaweb.com

International Executives Association is an elite business networking organization founded for one purpose: to share confidential business leads and information among its member firms. Executives Associations are in many major cities in the United States and Canada, as well as England, Switzerland, South Africa and beyond. Since 1916, Executives Associations have spread from city to city, started by business men and women sharing industry news with others, and seeking new ways to get an edge on their own competition. Today, there are over 110 official Executives Associations around the world. They make up the prestigious International Executives Association web, representing over 5,000 Member Firms.

P.O. Box 1997, Santa Rosa Beach, FL 32459, Tel: 850-622-1669, Fax: 813-354-3550

Email: director@ieaweb.com

Export/Import

American Importers Association

http://www.americanimporters.org

Their goal is to bring exporting companies from around the world together with American importing companies.

740 Sidney Marcus Blvd. Suite 4303, Atlanta, GA 30324, Tel: 404-317-7200, Fax: 404-846-9796 / 813-354-4619, Email: info@americanimporters.org

Export Institute of the United States of America

http://www.exportinstitute.com

They are dedicated to providing exporters around the world with the most practical and immediately usable information on selling their goods and services in foreign markets. We maintain continuous contact with trading companies large and small, universities, government agencies and entrepreneurs who have built successful export businesses.

6901 W.84th St., Suite 359, Minneapolis, MN 55438, Tel: 800-943-3171 / 952-943-1505, Fax: 952-943-1535, Email: jrj@exportinstitute.com

The International Import-Export Institute (IIEI)

http://ssadirat.tripod.com

The International Import-Export Institute (IIEI) is the international authority that certifies the proficiency of import-export trade professionals worldwide. With the assistance of advisors, college and university experts,

and members, IIEI develops and maintains the practical standards of excellence in the field of import-export management. Individuals who meet these high standards, as demonstrated by certification testing, are recognized with special distinction within the international business community.
P.O. Box 11378, Glendale, AZ 85318-1378, Tel: 800-474-8013 / 602-648-5750, Fax: 602-648-5755

Finance

Financial Executives Institute
http://www.fei.org/
FEI is the preeminent professional association for senior level financial executives, representing 15,000 individuals. Membership driven, FEI provides peer networking opportunities, emerging issues alerts, personal and professional development and advocacy services to Chief Financial Officers, VPs of Finance, Controllers, Treasurers, Tax Executives, Finance and Accounting Professors in academia. FEI does this principally through their strong Internet community, their 86 chapters and their 9 technical committees. Membership is limited to individuals holding senior management positions similar to those listed above, but FEI allows other finance professionals to join if they meet certain criteria.
Tel: 973-898-4600, Fax: 973-898-4649

Financial Management Association
http://www.fma.org/
The Financial Management Association International is a non-profit organization that publishes research and commentary on important financial issues; hosts an annual finance conference at which advances in theoretical and empirical research come together with the current issues and concerns of practicing finance professionals are taught, critiqued, and discussed; and brings together the professionals who share a common interest in finance.
University of South Florida, College of Business Administration, 4202 East Fowler Avenue, SN 331, Tampa FL 33620-5500, Tel: 813-974-2084, Fax: 813-974-3318

Franchise

International Franchise Association
http://www.franchise.org
The International Franchise Association protects, enhances and promotes franchising. 1350 New York Avenue NW Suite 900, Washington, D.C. 20005-4709, Tel: 202-628-8000, Fax: 202-628-0812, E-mail: ifa@franchise.org

Fundraising

Association of Fundraising Professionals
http://www.afpnet.org/
The Association of Fundraising Professionals (AFP) represents 26,000 members in 169 chapters throughout the United States, Canada and Mexico, working to advance philanthropy through advocacy, research, education.
1101 King Street Suite 700, Alexandria, VA 22314, Tel: 703-684-0410, Fax: 703-684-0540

Home-Based Business

American Association of Home-Based Businesses, Inc. (AAHBB)
http://www.aahbb.org
AAHBB's mission is to support, promote and encourage businesses in the home. P.O. Box 10023, Rockville, MD 20849, Tel: 888-823-2366, Fax: 301-963-7042, Email: aahbb@crosslink.net

Home Office Association of America
http://www.hoaa.com
Home Office Association of America is a six year old national organization dedicated to serving home-based and small business professionals.
P.O. Box 51, Sagaponack, NY 11962-0051, Tel: 800-809-4622 / 212-588-9097, Fax: 212-286-4646, E-mail: hoaa@aol.com

The National Association of Home Based Business (NAHBB)
http://www.ameribiz.com
The National Association of Home Based Businesses (NAHBB) has established an Intranet HomeSite System for home managed businesses. The U.S.A. Home Based Business Information Superhighway was estab-

lished to help home managed businesses, survive the shift to a global economy and to permit full participation now and in the 21st century. Intranet HomeSite System.
10451 Mill Run Circle Suite 400, Owings Mills, Maryland 21117, Tel: 410-363-3698, E-Mail: nahbb@msn.com

Home Building

National Association of Home Builders
http://www.nahb.com
NAHB exists to represent the building industry by serving its members and affiliated state and local builders associations.
1201 15th Street NW, Washington, DC 20005, Tel: 800-368-5242, Fax: 202-266-8559

Human Resources

International Association for Human Resource Information Management (IHRIM)
http://www.ihrim.org
The International Association for Human Resource Information Management (IHRIM) is your link to the unique world of HR information management, systems issues, trends, and technology.
P.O. Box 1086, Burlington, MA 01803-1086, Tel: 800-946-6363 / 512-453-6363, Fax: 781-998-8011, Email: moreinfo@ihrim.org

Society for Human Resource Management
www.shrm.org
The Society for Human Resource Management (SHRM) is the world's largest association devoted to human resource management. Representing more than 175,000 individual members, the Society's mission is to serve the needs of HR professionals by providing the most essential and comprehensive resources available. 1800 Duke Street Alexandria, Virginia 22314, Tel: (800) 283-SHRM.

Incubation

National Business Incubation Association
http://www.nbia.org
The National Business Incubation Association (NBIA) is the world's lead-

ing organization advancing business incubation and entrepreneurship. It provides thousands of professionals with the information, education, advocacy and networking resources to bring excellence to the process of assisting early-stage companies.
20 E. Circle Drive Suite 190, Athens, OH 45701-3571, Tel: 740-593-4331, Fax: 740-593-1996, Email: info@nbia.org

Information Technology

Association of Internet Professionals
http://www.association.org/
Representing more than 9,500 individual Internet Professionals and over 150 leading Internet industry companies and educational institutions, The Association of Internet Professionals (AIP) is the premier professional association of the Internet industry.
The AIP exists to unify, support and represent the global community of Internet professionals. The organization also serves as a forum for the ideas, people and issues shaping the future of the Internet industry.
4790 Irvine Boulevard Suite 105-283, Irvine, CA 92620, Tel: 866-AIP-9700, Fax: 501-423-2248, Email: info@association.org

Business Software Alliance
http://www.bsa.org/
Since 1988, the Business Software Alliance (BSA) has been the voice of the world's leading software developers before governments and with consumers in the international marketplace. Its members represent the fastest growing industry in the world. BSA educates computer users on software copyrights; advocates public policy that fosters innovation and expands trade opportunities; and fights software piracy.
1150 18th Street, N.W. Suite 700, Washington, D.C. 20036, Tel: 202-872-5500, Fax: 202-872-5501, Email: software@bsa.org

Computing Technology Industry Association
http://www.comptia.org/
The computing and communications industries continue to grow at a staggering rate. And with the growth come new rewards and challenges. We work to develop vendor-neutral standards in -commerce, customer service, workforce development, and training certification.
1815 S. Meyers Road Suite 300, Oakbrook Terrace, IL 60181-5228, Tel: 630-678-8300, Fax: 630-268-1384

emarketing Assocation
http://www.emarketingassociation.com/
The eMarketing Association (eMA) is the professional association for companies and individuals involved in the practice of e-marketing and the integration of on-line and offline marketing. The eMA is a premier resource for web certifications, professional certifications, seminars, events, processes, trade shows, news, standards, advertising, techniques, and trends. They are committed to enriching their members through recognition, research, advocacy education, and service.
2110 Artesia Blvd. 347, Redondo Beach, CA 90278, Tel: 800 -417-7506, Fax: 408-884-2461

Internet Advertising Bureau
http://www.iab.net
The IAB is the only association dedicated to helping online, Interactive broadcasting, email, wireless and Interactive television media companies increase their revenues.
1440 Broadway 21st Floor, New York, NY 10018, Tel: 212-949-9033

International Webmasters Association
http://www.iwanet.org/
Provide and foster professional advancement opportunities among individuals dedicated to or pursuing a Web career, and to work diligently to enhance their effectiveness, image, and professionalism as they attract and serve their clients and employers.
119 E. Union Street Suite #F, Pasadena, California 91103, Tel: 626-449-3709, Fax: 626-449-8308

World Technology Network
http://www.wtn.net
Encourage emerging technologies by bringing together key players from diverse disciplines: technology, finance, marketing, government, events and membership.
74 Chelsea Manor Street, London SW3 5QD, United Kingdom, Tel: 44-0-20-7349-0826, Fax: 44-0-20-7352-5318, Email: info@wtn.net

Insurance

American Insurance Association
http://www.aiadc.org/
The American Insurance Association (AIA) is a property/casualty insurance trade association. It has existed for more than 125 years and represents over 250 property and casualty insurance companies.
1130 Connecticut Ave NW Ste.1000, Washington, DC 20036, Tel: 202-828-7100, Fax: 202-293-1219, Email: membership@aiadc.org

International Management

Association of Career Professionals International
http://www.acpinternational.org
The Association of Career Professionals International is the World's Voice on Career Issues. With more than 2000 members who bring global expertise from both independent practices and large firms, they are represented in more than 30 countries around the world.
204 E Street NE, Washington, DC 20002, Tel: 202-547-6377, Fax: 202-547-6348, Email: info@acpinternational.org

Business Council for International Understanding
http://www.bciu.org
BCIU is a business association founded in 1959 at the initiative of the Eisenhower Administration. Through its work, BCIU helps dues-paying members succeed in today's global business arena by facilitating dialogue and action between business and government.
Worldwide Headquarters:
1212 Avenue of the Americas 10th Floor, New York, NY 10036, Tel: 212-490-0460, Fax: 212-697-8526

The National Association of Foreign-Trade Zones (NAFTZ)
http://www.naftz.org
The National Association of Foreign-Trade Zones (NAFTZ) is a non-profit organization composed of public entities, individuals and corporations involved in the U.S. Foreign-Trade Zones program. The NAFTZ Promotes the use of the Foreign-Trade Zones program to facilitate and increase the global competitiveness of U.S. based companies
1000 Connecticut Avenue NW Suite 1001, Washington, DC 20036, Tel: 202-331-1950, Fax: 202-331-1994, Email: info@naftz.org

World Trade Organization
http://www.wto.org/
The WTO is the only international body dealing with the rules of trade between nations. At its heart are the WTO agreements, the legal ground-rules for international commerce and for trade policy. The agreements have three main objectives: to help trade flow as freely as possible, to achieve further liberalization gradually through negotiation, and to set up an impartial means of settling disputes.
Centre William Rappard, Rue de Lausanne 154, CH-1211 Geneva 21, Switzerland, Tel: 41-22-739-51-11, Fax: 41-22-731-42-06, Email: enquiries@wto.org

Invention

National Congress of Inventor Organizations
http://www.inventionconvention.com/ncio
Resource for inventors and entrepreneurs. Inventor Online magazine, free consultations, patent search online, links to patent office and other government resources, free how-to information on how to keep proper records, important warning information about invention scams.
P.O. Box 93669, Los Angeles, CA 90093-6690, USA, Tel: 888-695-4455 / 323-878-6952, Fax: 213-947-1079, Email: ncio@inventionconvention.com

Law

American Bar Association
www.abanet.org
Welcome to the American Bar Association, the largest voluntary professional association in the world. With more than 400,000 members, the ABA provides law school accreditation, continuing legal education, information about the law, programs to assist lawyers and judges in their work, and initiatives to improve the legal system for the public. 541 N. Fairbanks Ct Chicago, IL 60611, 312.988.5522, 800-285-2221

Leadership /Management

American Management Association
http://www.amanet.org/
American Management Association is the world's leading membership-based management development and training organization. Information

and resources are available on all aspects of business management and professional development. 1601 Broadway New York, NY 10019, Tel: 212-586-8100, Fax: 212-903-8168,
Email: customerservice@amanet.org

Business Enterprise Trust
http://www.betrust.org/index.html
The Business Enterprise Trust is a national, non-profit organization that promotes social leadership in business. Through the annual Business Enterprise Awards, the Trust honors business heroes who creatively combine sound management with social conscience. This site provides information about the organization, its awards, educational material, and board and staff members.

The Conference Board
http://www.conference-board.org/
The Conference Board is the world's leading business membership and research organization, connecting senior executives from more than 2,200 enterprises in over 60 nations. A nonprofit, nonadvocacy organization, The Conference Board produces the Consumer Confidence Index, the Leading Economic Indicators, and a wide range of reports on best business practices and the latest economic trends, which leads to The Conference Board receiving more than 21,000 media citations per year. The Conference Board also provides a diverse program of conferences and forums for over 15,000 executives from different industries and nations to meet and share insights.
845 Third Avenue, New York, NY 10022, Tel: 212-339-0345, Fax: 212-836-9740

Institute of Management Consultants
http://www.imcusa.org/
Founded in 1968, the Institute of Management Consultants (IMC) is the leading association representing management consultants with members in the U.S. and overseas. Through combined efforts by the principal associations and societies in the field, IMC represents management consulting as a self-regulating profession, meriting the same public confidence and respect as medicine, accounting or law.
2025 M Street N. W. Suite 800, Washington, DC 20036-3309, Tel: 202-367-1134 800-221-2557, Fax: 202-367-2134, Email: office@imcusa.org

Marketing / Advertising /Sales

Association of National Advertisers

http://www.ana.net/default.htm

The Association of National Advertisers are the industry's premier marketing and advertising trade association, the only organization exclusively dedicated to serving the interests of corporations that advertise and market their products and services in the U.S. Founded in 1910, they are headquartered in New York City.

708 Third Avenue, New York, NY 10017-4270, Tel: 212-697-5950, Fax: 212-661-8057

The Ad Council

http://www.adcouncil.org/

For 55 years, the Ad Council has created the timely and compelling public service messages Americans needed to hear. Along the way, The Ad Council has given our culture some of its most enduring slogans and characters, Smokey Bear to name but one. But their slogans and characters are more than memorable - they raise awareness, inspire action, and save lives. The Ad Council uses the power of advertising to stimulate action against the problems confronting Americans today. They are joined in this mission by the media, the advertising industry, the business world and the non-profit community.

261 Madison Avenue 11th Floor, New York, NY 10016, Tel: 212-922-1500, Fax: 212-922-1676, Email: info@adcouncil.org

American Advertising Federation

http://www.aaf.org/

The American Advertising Federation (AAF) is The Unifying Voice for Advertising. They are the only professional advertising association that binds the mutual interests of corporate advertisers, agencies, media companies, suppliers and academia. The AAF's 50,000 members share a commitment to make advertising a positive force in America's economy and culture. They are advocates for the rights of advertisers and we educate policymakers, the news media and the general public on the value that advertising brings to the well-being of the nation.

1101 Vermont Avenue NW Suite 500, Washington, DC 20005-6306, Tel: 202-898-0089, Fax: 202-898-0159, Email: aaf@aaf.org

American Marketing Association
http://www.ama.org/
The American Marketing Association is an international professional organization for people involved in the practice, study and teaching of marketing.
311 S. Wacker Dr. Suite# 5800 Chicago, Ill. 60606, Tel: 312-542-9070, Fax: 912-542-9001, Email: info@ama.org

American Wholesale Marketers Association
http://www.awmanet.org/
The American Wholesale Marketers Association (AWMA) is a non-profit, national trade association serving more than 3,000 companies involved in the distribution, manufacture and retail sale of convenience products. Members consist of wholesalers, manufacturers, retailers, brokers and others involved in the convenience products industry. From maker to market, the association has benefits and services to fill every channel member's needs.
1128 16th St. NW, Washington DC 20036, Tel: 800-482-2962, Fax: 202-463-2124, Email: info@awmanet.org

Direct Marketing Association
http://www.the-dma.org/
Founded in 1917, the Direct Marketing Association (The DMA) is the oldest and largest trade association for users and suppliers in the direct, database and interactive marketing field.
1120 Avenue of the Americas, New York, NY 10036-6700, Tel: 212-768-7277, Fax: 212-302-6714, Email: consumer@the-dma.org

Direct Selling Association
http://www.dsa.org/
The Direct Selling Association (DSA) is the national trade association of the leading firms that manufacture and distribute goods and services sold directly to consumers. More than 150 companies are members of the association, including many well-known brand names.
1275 Pennsylvania Avenue NW Suite 800, Washington, DC 20004, Tel: 202-347-8866, Fax: 202-347-0055, Email: info@dsa.org

International Advertising Association
http://www.iaaglobal.org/
The International Advertising Association is the only global partnership of advertisers, agencies and media, representing over 3400 members in 87

countries.
521 Fifth Avenue Suite 1807, New York, NY 10175, Tel: 212-557-1133, Fax: 212-983-0455, Email: iaa@iaaglobal.org

Internet Advertising Bureau
http://www.iab.net/
The Internet Advertising Bureau (IAB) is the only industry association devoted exclusively to promoting the use and effectiveness of advertising on the Internet. General members include companies that are actively engaged in the sales of advertising. The organization membership also consists of companies that support advertising sales activities such as measurement companies, research suppliers, traffic companies and organizations from related industries.
1440 Broadway 21st Floor, New York, NY 10018, Tel: 212-949-9034

Marketing Research Association
http://www.mra-net.org/
MRA promotes excellence in the opinion and marketing research industry by providing members with a variety of opportunities for advancing and expanding their marketing research and related business skills. To protect the marketing research environment, we will act as an advocate with appropriate government entities, other associations, and the public.
1344 Silas Deane Hwy. Suite 306, P.O. Box 230, Rocky Hill, CT 06067-0230, Tel: 860-257-4008, Fax: 860-257-3990, Email: email@mra-net.org

National Association of Sales Professionals
http://www.nasp.com
This organization keeps a network of sales professionals from all over the country.
NASP encourages international participation by those who are interested in obtaining a professional sales certification. NASP is comprised of dynamic men and women who have distinguished themselves as leaders in the rapidly changing world of sales. They have committed to advancing their job and financial security by earning recognition as a Certified Professional SalesPersonTM (CPSP)
8300 North Hayden Road Suite 207, Scottsdale, AZ 85258, Tel: 480-951-4311, Fax: 602-263-0515, Email: millar@nasp.com

National Mail Order Association

http://www.nmoa.org/

The National Mail Order Association is a 27 year old organization that provides education, information and contacts to the direct marketing industry. It's main focus is helping small to midsize companies.

2807 Polk St. NE, Minneapolis, MN 55418-2954, Tel: 612-788-1673, Fax: 612-788-1147, Email: info@nmoa.org

Sales and Marketing Executives International

http://www.smei.org

Professional Identification and Standards. The improvement of the standards for professional selling, sales management and marketing, in order to establish sales and marketing as a recognized profession.

P.O. Box 1390 9 - 32442, Dahlstrom Ave, Sumas, WA 98295-1390, Tel: 312-893-0751, Fax: 604-855-0165

World Federation of Direct Selling Associations

http://www.wfdsa.org

Mission is to support direct selling associations in the areas of governance, education, communications, consumer protection, and ethics in the marketplace. News, legal compendium, and position papers are available at this site.

1275 Pennsylvania Avenue NW Suite 800, Washington, DC 20004, Tel: 202-347-8866, Fax: 202-347-0055, Email: info@wfdsa.org

Manufacturing

National Association of Manufacturers

http://www.nam.org

The NAM's mission is to enhance the competitiveness of manufacturers and to improve American living standards by shaping a legislative and regulatory environment conducive to U.S. economic growth, and to increase understanding among policymakers, the media and the general public about the importance of manufacturing to America's economic strength.

The National Association of Manufacturers - 18 million

1331 Pennsylvania Ave. NW, Washington, DC 20004-1790, Tel: 202-637-3000, Fax: 202-637-3182, Email: manufacturing@nam.org

Meeting /Event

Meeting Planners International
www.mpiweb.org
Established in 1972, Meeting Professionals International (MPI) is the leading global community committed to shaping and defining the future of the meeting and event industry. As the largest trade association for the $102.3 billion meeting industry, MPI defines the return on investment and strategic value meetings bring to individuals, organizations and the global economy. MPI helps its members enhance their professional value by providing them with best practices, superior education, the latest research and trends, professional development and networking opportunities.
4455 LBJ Freeway, Suite 1200 Dallas, Texas, 75244-5903 Voice: +1-972-702-3000

MBA

Association of MBAs
http://www.mba.org.uk/
The Association of MBAs is unique in representing the interests of MBA students and graduates, leading business schools and MBA employers. The Association has acted in the interests of these stakeholder groups for over 30 years, promoting the MBA as the leading management qualification. Our aim is to encourage management education at postgraduate level to create highly competent professional managers.
15 Duncan Terrace, London N1 8BZ, United Kingdom, Tel: + 44-0-20-7837-3375, Fax: +44-0-20-7278-3634, Email: Info@mba.org.uk

National Black MBA Association, Inc.
http://www.nbmbaa.org/
The National Black MBA Association, Inc. (NBMBAA) is a non-profit organization of minority MBAs, business professionals, entrepreneurs and MBA students. With close to 5,000 members working in both private and public sectors throughout the country, we share a commitment to education and business -- the two principal keys to the economic development of the African American community.
180 Michigan Ave. Suite 1400, Chicago, IL 60601, Tel: 312-236-2622, Fax: 312-236-4131, Email: mail@nbmbaa.org

National Society of Hispanic MBAs
http://www.nshmba.org/
The premier Hispanic MBA professional business network for economic and philanthropic advancement fostering Hispanic leadership through graduate management education and professional development in order to improve society.
1303 Walnut Hill Lane Suite 300, Irving, TX 75038, Tel: 877-467-4622, Fax: 214-596-9325

199 South Monte Vista Avenue Suite 6, San Dimas, CA 91773, Tel: 800-825-8286 / 909-305-1818, Fax: 909-305-1811

Non-Profit

National Council of Nonprofit Associations
http://www.ncna.org
The largest state-by-state alliance of nonprofits in the United States, NCNA is a network of 40 state and regional associations with a collective membership of more than 20,000 community nonprofits. NCNA publishes State Tax Trends, a quarterly newsletter that reports on state and local tax issues, and Field Notes, a series of case studies on innovative program initiatives carried out by state and regional associations of nonprofit organizations.
1030 15th Street NW Suite 870, Washington, DC 20005, Tel: 202-962-0322, Fax: 202-962-0321, Email: ncna@ncna.org

Association for Research on Nonprofit Organizations and Voluntary Action (ARNOVA)
http://www.u.washington.edu
The Association for Research on Nonprofit Organizations and Voluntary Action (ARNOVA) is an international, interdisciplinary membership organization. Its members include scholars and nonprofit leaders fostering the creation, application and dissemination of research on voluntary action, nonprofit organizations, philanthropy and civil society.
550 West North St. Suite 301, Indianapolis, IN 46202-3272, Tel: 317-684-2120, Fax: 317-684-2128, Email: nvsq@u.washington.edu

The Management Assistance Program for Nonprofits
http://www.mapnp.org/
Founded in 1979, MAP, The Management Assistance Program for

Nonprofits, is a nonprofit management support agency that provides affordable consulting, leadership and technical assistance to other charitable nonprofit organizations primarily within Minneapolis and St. Paul, Minnesota. MAP recruits employed and retired professionals to volunteer to clients as consultants or board members. MAP hosts Carter McNamara's Managers Free Library to help provide highly accessible and practical resources to managers throughout the nation
2233 University Avenue West Suite 360, St Paul, MN 55114-1629, Tel: 651-647-1216, Fax: 651-647-1369, Email to: mail@mapnp.org

Office Related

Home Office Association of America

http://www.hoaa.com
The Home Office Association of America is a six year old national organization dedicated to serving home-based and small business professionals.
P.O. Box 51, Sagaponack, NY 11962-0051, Tel: 212-588-9097 / 800-809-4622, Fax: 212-286-4646, Email: hoaa@aol.com

International Association of Virtual Office Assistants (IAVOA)

http://www.iavoa.com
The purpose of the International Association of Virtual Office Assistants (IAVOA) is to promote the use of Virtual Assistants Worldwide. Provide those organizations that want to utilize the services of a VA the best possible forum and support available anywhere in the world.
Route 1 Box 275, Red Oak, OK 74563, Tel: 918-753-2716, Fax: 918-753-2717 Email: iavoa@aol.com

Organizational Development

National Association of Development Organizations (NADO)

http://www.nado.org
The National Association of Development Organizations (NADO) provides training, information and representation for regional development organizations in small metropolitan and rural America. The association, a public interest group founded in 1967, is the largest and leading advocate for a regional approach to community, economic and rural development and provides a network for its members to share ideas and innovations.
400 North Capitol St. NW Suite 390, Washington, DC 20001, Tel: 202-624-7806, Fax: 202-624-8813, Email: info@nado.org

Outdoor

Outdoor Industry Association
http://outdoorindustry.org/
To promote and preserve the human-powered outdoor recreation industry. 3775 Iris Avenue Suite 5, Boulder, CO 80301, Tel: 303-444-3353, Fax: 303-444-3284, Email: info@outdoorindustry.org

Project Management

Project Management Institute
http://www.pmi.org/
Founded in 1969, PMI is the leading nonprofit professional association in the area of Project Management. PMI establishes Project Management standards, provides seminars, educational programs and professional certification that more and more organizations desire for their project leaders. Four Campus Blvd, Newtown Square, PA 19073-3299, Tel: 610-356-4600, Fax: 610-356-4647, Email: pmihq@pmi.org

Psychology / Counseling

American Counseling Association
www.counseling.org

The American Counseling Association is a not-for-profit, professional and educational organization that is dedicated to the growth and enhancement of the counseling profession. Founded in 1952, ACA is the world's largest association exclusively representing professional counselors in various practice settings.
By providing leadership training, publications, continuing education opportunities, and advocacy services to nearly 52,000 members, ACA helps counseling professionals develop their skills and expand their knowledge base.

5999 Stevenson Ave. Alexandria, VA 22304 Tel: (800) 347-6647

American Psychological Association
www.apa.org
Based in Washington, DC, the American Psychological Association (APA) is a scientific and professional organization that represents psychology in

the United States. With more than 150,000 members, APA is the largest association of psychologists worldwide.
750 First Street, NE, Washington, DC 20002-4242
Telephone: 800-374-2721; 202-336-5510. TDD/TTY: 202-336-6123

Public Relations

Public Relations Society of America
http://www.prsa.org/
The Public Relations Society of America, headquartered in New York City, is the world's largest professional organization for public relations practitioners
33 Irving Place, New York, NY 10003-2376, Tel: 212-995-2230, Fax: 212-995-0757, Email: membership@prsa.org

Publishing / Journalism

American Society of Journalists and Authors
http://www.asja.org/
Founded in 1948, the American Society of Journalists and Authors is the nation's leading organization of independent nonfiction writers. Its membership consists of more than 1,000 outstanding freelance writers of magazine articles, trade books, and many other forms of nonfiction writing, each of whom has met ASJA's exacting standards of professional achievement.
1501 Broadway, Suite 302, New York, NY 10036, (212) 997-0947_

Association of American Publishers
www.publishers.org
To expand the market for American books and other published works in all media;
To promote the status of publishing in the United States and throughout the world;
To nurture creativity by protecting and strengthening intellectual property rights, especially copyright; To foster public understanding of the unique value of books and other published materials in the cultural and political life of our nation. 71 Fifth Avenue, 2nd Floor, New York, NY 10003, Phone: 212/255-0200

Writers Guild of America

www.wgaeast.org

The Writers Guild, East is a labor union protecting and defending the rights of the men and women who write, illustrate and produce the news and information programming for TV, radio and all other electronic media. And they also represent screenwriters and entertainment TV writers. 555 West 57th Street, Suite 1230 New York, NY 10019, Tel: (212) 767-7800

Purchasing Management

National Association of Purchasing Management

http://www.napm.org/

The National Association of Purchasing Management has fostered national and international leadership in purchasing and materials management since 1915. A not-for-profit organization, NAPM cultivates programming, networking, and professional development opportunities for a growing body of more than 40,000 members.

P.O. Box 22160, Tempe, AZ 85285-2160, Tel: 480-752-6276 / 800-888-6276, Fax: 480-752-7890

Quality Management

American Society for Quality

http://www.asq.org/

ASQ is a society of individual and organizational members dedicated to the ongoing, development, advancement, and promotion of quality concepts, principles, and techniques.

600 North Plankinton Avenue, Milwaukee, WI 53203, Tel: 800-248-1946 / 414-272-8575, Fax: 414-272-1734, Email: help@asq.org

Real Estate

National Association of Realtors

http://nar.realtor.com/

The National Association of Realtors is the nation's largest trade and professional association representing nearly 750,000 members. It is composed of residential and commercial realtors. Westlake Village, CA 91362, Tel: 805-557-2300, Fax: 805-557-2680

Research

Council of American Survey Research Organizations
http://www.casro.org
The Council of American Survey Research Organizations (CASRO) is the trade association of survey research businesses, representing nearly 200 companies and research operations in the United States, Canada, and Mexico.
3 Upper Devon, Port Jefferson, New York 11777, USA, Tel: 631-928-6954 - Fax: 631-928-6041
Email: casro@casro.org

Resources

American Evaluation Association
http://www.eval.org/
We are an international professional association of evaluators devoted to the application and exploration of program evaluation, personnel evaluation, technology, and many other forms of evaluation. Evaluation involves assessing the strengths and weaknesses of programs, policies, personnel, products, and organizations to improve their effectiveness."
16 Sconticut Neck Rd #290, Fairhaven, MA 02719, Tel - Fax: 888-232-2275 / 508-748-3326, Email: AEA@kistcon.com

Retail

National Retail Federation
http://www.nrf.com/
As the world's largest retail trade association, NRF's mission is to conduct programs and services in research, education, training, information technology, and government affairs to protect and advance the interests of the retail industry. NRF's membership includes the leading department, specialty, independent, discount, and mass merchandise stores in the United States and 50 nations around the world. NRF represents more than 100 state, national and international trade organizations, which have members in most lines of retailing. NRF also includes in its membership key suppliers of goods and services to the retail industry.
325 7th Street, NW Suite 1100, Washington, DC 20004, Tel: 202-783-7971 / 800-NRF-HOW2, Fax: 202-737-2849

Security

Society of Registered Securities Professionals
http://www.srsp.org
To work cooperatively with their members and all of society to research and publicize the best information on the art of wealth management and of the ethical principles that should guide it so that registered representatives are recognized as the ultimate professionals in the art.
100 West Old Wilson Bridge Rd Suite 101, Worthington, OH 43085, Tel: 800-877-0083, Fax: 614-436-1528, Email: srsp@netwalk.com

National Business Association
http://www.nationalbusiness.org
The National Business Association (NBA) is a not for profit association, specifically designed and actively managed to assist the Self-Employed and Small Business Community in achieving their professional goals.P.O. Box 700728, Dallas, Texas 75370, Tel: 800-456-0440 / 972-458-0900, Fax: 972-960-9149, Email: info@nationalbusiness.org

National Federation of Independent Business (NFIB)
http://www.nfibonline.com
NFIB, the National Federation of Independent Business, is the largest advocacy organization representing small and independent businesses in Washington, D.C. and all 50 state capitals.
Tel: 800-NFIB-NOW

National Small Business United (NSBU)
http://www.nsbu.biz
National Small Business United is the nation's oldest bipartisan advocate for small businesses. Representing over 65,000 small business owners, NSBU takes action on legislative and regulatory issues by playing a key role in shaping federal policy in the interests of small business. Their main goal is to protect and promote our members and all 23 million small businesses before the Congress and the Administration. 1156 15th Street NW Suite 1100, Washington, DC 20005, Tel: 202-293-8830, Fax: 202-872-8543, Email: nsbu@nsbu.org

Tax

National Association of Tax Professionals

http://www.natptax.com/

The National Association of Tax Professionals (NATP), founded in 1979, is a nonprofit professional association dedicated to excellence in taxation. NATP was formed to serve professionals who work in all areas of tax practice. Members include CPAs, individual practitioners, enrolled agents, accountants, attorneys, and financial planners.

720 Association Drive, Appleton, WI 54914-1483, Tel: 800-558-3402, Fax: 800-747-0001, Email: natp@natptax.com

Trade

The Federation of International Trade Associations

http://www.fita.org

FITA's goal for this site is to provide the most content-rich international trade site and to provide a comprehensive global trade shop featuring goods and services needed by those involved in international trade.

11800 Sunrise Valley Drive Suite 210, Reston, VA 20191, Tel: 800-969-3482 / 703-620-1588, Fax: 703-622-4922, Email: info@fita.org

Training and Development

American Society for Training and Development

http://www.astd.org

Founded in 1944, ASTD is the world's premier professional association and leading resource on workplace learning and performance issues. ASTD provides information, research, analysis and practical information derived from its own research, the knowledge and experience of its members, its conferences, expositions, seminars, publications and the coalitions and partnerships it has built through research and policy work. ASTD's membership includes more than 70,000 people, working in the field of workplace performance in 100 countries worldwide.

1640 King Street, Box 1443, Alexandria, Virginia, 22313-2043, Tel: 703-683-8100, Fax: 703-683-8103

Women Organizations

American Association of University Women (AAUW)
http://www.aauw.org
A national organization that promotes education and equality for all women and girls. Mission: AAUW promotes equity for all women and girls, lifelong education, and positive societal change. 1111 Sixteenth St. N.W. Washington, DC 20036
Tel: 800/326-AAUW, Fax: 202/872-1425, TDD: 202/785-7777
E-mail: info@aauw.org

American Business Women's Association
http://www.abwa.org
To bring together businesswomen of diverse occupations and to provide opportunities for them to help themselves and others grow personally and professionally through leadership, education, networking support and national recognition.
Ms. Angela Eastin, President, 79 Locust Avenue #222, New Canaan, CT 06840, Tel: 203-358-3703, Fax: 203-358-5816, E-mail: eastina@aol.com

American Society of Women Accountants
http://www.aswa.org
ASWA was formed in 1938 to increase the opportunities for women in all fields of accounting and finance. The mission of ASWA is to enable women in all accounting and related fields to achieve their full personal, professional and economic potential and to contribute to the future development of their profession.
8405 Greensboro Drive Suite 800, McLean, VA 22102, Tel: 800-326-2163 / 703-506-3265, Fax: 703-506-3266, Email: aswa@aswa.org

Association of Women in Communications
www.womcom.org
The Association for Women in Communications is the one organization that recognizes the complex relationships that exist across communications disciplines. Modern communicators must demonstrate competence in varied disciplines and be able to network and make career moves across the broad spectrum of communications fields.
Disciplines represented within the association include: print and broadcast journalism, television and radio production, film, advertising, public relations, marketing, graphic design, multi-media design, and photography. The list is continually growing as the profession expands into the newer

media.
780 Ritchie Highway, Suite 28-S, Severna Park, MD 21146 Phone: 410-544-7442

Aurora Women's Network
http://www.auroravoice.com/
Aurora works for the economic advancement of women, benchmarking gender
capital across industry through their www.www2wk.com initiative, and delivers a 15,000 international corporate and entrepreneurial women's network. Aurora Gender Capital Management
Albert Buildings
49 Queen Victoria Street
London EC4N 4SA
United Kingdom Telephone: +44 (0) 20 7653 1909

Asian Women in Business
Asian Women in Business is a not-for-profit membership organization founded in 1995 to assist Asian women to realize their entrepreneurial potential.
http://www.awib.org
Asian Women in Business
358 Fifth Avenue, Suite 504
New York, NY 10001

Association for Professional Insurance Women
http://www.apiw.org/
The APIW is a professional association of women. APIW members are highly regarded decision-makers with primary insurers, reinsurers, insurance brokers, risk management, professional services firms and other industry-related organizations
P.O. Box 9001, Mt. Vernon, NY 10552, Tel: 914-699-2020 ext 115 or 128, Fax: 914-699-2025, Email: Info@apiw.org

Association for Women in Computing
http://www.iwanet.org/
The Association for Women in Computing is a non-profit professional organization for women and men who have an interest in information and technology. The Association is dedicated to the advancement of women in the technology fields.

41 Sutter Street Suite 1006, San Francisco, California 94104, Tel: 415-905-4663 awc@awc-hq.org

Association for Women's Rights in Development (AWID)
http://www.awid.org
The Association for Women's Rights in Development (AWID) is an international membership organization connecting, informing and mobilizing people and organizations committed to achieving gender equality, sustainable development and women's human rights. AWIDs goal is to cause policy, institutional and individual change that will improve the lives of women and girls everywhere. They do this by facilitating ongoing debates on fundamental and provocative issues as well as by building the individual and organizational capacities of those working for women's empowerment and social justice.
96 Spadina Ave. Suite 401, Toronto, ON Canada M5V 2J6, Tel: 416-594-3773, Fax: 416-594-0330, Email: awid@awid.org

Business Women Connect
http://www.BusinessWomenConnect.com
Indy Business Women Connect provides networking opportunities for women.
8470 Allison Point Blvd. #100 Indianapolis, Indiana 46250 317-713-6815, Email: Linda@BusinessWomenConnect.com.

Canadian Women's Business Network (CWBN)
An established online network for women designed to help them build their business. Participation in this network isn't limited to business owners. Women in management, sales, etc. can benefit from the exposure they receive on CWBN and are welcome to join.
http://www.cdnbizwomen.com
(250) 751-2133
Canadian Women's Business Network
3019 Hammond Bay Road
Nanaimo, BC, Canada V9T 1E1

Catalyst
http://www.catalystwomen.org
Catalyst is the nonprofit research and advisory organization working to advance women in business and the professions, with offices in New York and Toronto. The leading source of information on women in business for the past four decades, Catalyst has the knowledge and tools that help

companies and women maximize their potential. Their solutions-oriented approach through research, Advisory Services, Corporate Board Placement, the Catalyst Award, and Member Services has earned the confidence of global business leaders. The American Institute of Philanthropy consistently ranks Catalyst as the highest rated nonprofit in the US focused on women's issues.
New York Office
120 Wall Street, 5th Floor
New York, New York 10005
p: (212) 514-7600
f: (212) 514-8470
e: info@catalystwomen.org

Center for Women's Business Research
Founded as The National Association for Women Business Owners
The Center for Women's Business Research, founded as the National Foundation for Women Business Owners, is the premier source of knowledge about women business owners and their enterprises worldwide.
http://www.nfwbo.org
To speak with someone directly about partnering with the Center for Women's Business Research, please contact Rena Pina at 202-638-3060 ext. 20

Committee of 200
The Committee of 200 is the professional organization of preeminent women entrepreneurs and corporate leaders. The organization capitalizes on the power, success and influence of businesswomen in the global economy.
http://www.c200.org
980 N. Michigan Avenue
Suite 1575,
Chicago, IL 60611 USA
Ph: (312) 255-0296
Fax: (312) 255-0789

eWomen Network, Inc
www.ewomennetwork.com
At eWomenNetwork.com our vision is a vast network of female business owners and professionals all connected to each other. We want success-minded women to have easy access to each other's skills, talents, knowl-

edge and resources.
14900 Landmark Boulevard Suite 540, Dallas, TX, 75254, Tel: 972-620-9995, Fax: 972-720-9995, Email: info@ewomennetwork.com

Home Based Working Moms

The goal of HBWM.com, Inc. is to help moms create lifestyles that enable them more freedom and flexibility to truly enjoy their family and their life.
http://www.hbwm.com/
PO Box 500164
Austin, TX 78750
Phone: 512.266.0900
Email: hbwm @hbwm.com

International Women's Forum

The IWF is a global organization of preeminent women of significant and diverse achievement. Members come together across national and international boundaries to share knowledge and ideas, to enrich each other's lives, to provide a network of support and to exert influence. Through the Leadership Foundation, the International Women's Forum helps prepare future generations of women leaders.
http://www.iwforum.org
1424 16th Street, NW
Suite 105
Washington, DC 20036
Telephone: (202) 387-1010
Fax: (202) 387-1009
Email: iwf@iwforum.org

Hong Kong Association of Business and Professional Women

http://www.hkabpw.org

Organization of working women, who have actively promoted the interests of business and professional women in Hong Kong since 1979.

National Association for Female Executives

http://www.nafe.com
The National Association for Female Executives (NAFE), the largest women's professional association and the largest women business owners' organization in the country, provides resources and services - through education, networking, and public advocacy - to empower its members to

achieve career success and financial security.
P.O. Box 469031, Escondido, CA 92046-9925, Tel: 800-634-NAFE

National Council of Women's Organizations
http://www.womensorganizations.org
The National Council of Women's Organizations is a nonpartisan network of more than one hundred women's organizations, which together represent more than 6 million members.
733 15th Street. NW Suite 1011, Washington, DC 20005, Tel: 202-393-7122, Fax: 202-387-7915, E-mail: info@womensorganizations.org

National Women's Business Council
http://www.iwanet.org/
The National Women's Business Council is a bi-partisan Federal government council created to serve as an independent source of advice and counsel to the President, Congress, U.S. Small Business Administration, and the Interagency Committee on Women's Business on economic issues of importance to women business owners. Members of the Council are prominent women business owners and leaders of women's business organizations. The mission of the Council is to promote initiatives, policies and programs designed to support women's business enterprises at all stages of development in the public and private sector marketplaces.
409 3rd Street, S.W. Suite 210, Washington, DC 20024, USA, Tel: 202-205-3850 - Fax: 202-205-6825, Email: nwbc@sba.gov

Organization of Woman In International Trade
http://www.owit.org/
The Organization of Women in International Trade (OWIT) is "a non-profit professional organization designed to promote women doing business in international trade by providing networking and educational opportunities. Its members include women and men doing business in all facets of international trade including finance, public relations, government, freight forwarding, international law, agriculture, sales and marketing, import/export, logistics, and transportation.
Chapter President & OWIT Representative, Janet Day Richey, 170 L Street, Boston, MA 02127, Tel: 617-464-1406, Fax: 617-464-0033

Paris Professional Women's Network
A network of professional women based in Paris. The group's objective is to facilitate the exchange of ideas, enhance networking and encourage

mutual support.
http://www.parispwn.net
ParisPWN
126, rue de Canotiers
78670 Villennes sur Seine
Phone: 06 89 63 09 82
E-mail: info@parispwn.net

WITI

For more than a decade, WITI has successfully provided women in technology inspiration, education, conferences, on-line services, publications and an exceptional worldwide network of resources. WITI is the first and only international organization solely dedicated to advancing women through technology.
http://www.witi.com
13351-D Riverside Drive #441
Sherman Oaks, CA 91423
Phone: 800.334.WITI
Voice: 818.788.9484
Fax: 818.896.4746

Women's Council of Realtors

http://www.wcr.org/
The Women's Council of Realtors (WCR) is a professional association for female real estate professionals. It was established in 1938 and currently has 13,000 members.
430 North Michigan Avenue, Chicago, IL 60611, Email: wcrweb@wcr.org

World WIT

http://www.worldwit.org/index.html
WorldWIT.org is a global, online community for women in technology. That means technical women, and other women involved in the 'tech sector,' including entrepreneurs, venture capitalists, sales/marketing/bizdev folks, consultants, educators, journalists, freelancers and attorneys. They provide a free, friendly resource for women in the form of information and advice from other members of our community. WorldWIT, Inc. 3405 Penrose Place Suite 100 Boulder, CO 80301 (303) 442-1482

Glossary of Terms

How to use The Glossary

The words listed in this glossary will help you better understand our intent of word usage throughout the book. While Webster's dictionary is always a good source for word definition, in many instances, we have provided a slant on the interpretation and the contemporary meaning of words.

This glossary can be used in the following ways:

1 Search out the word definition to heighten your understanding as needed.

2 Read the entire glossary as a way to develop a relationship mind set.

3 Strengthen your understanding of a NetBeing philosophy.

A

ACT - A computer software program for tracking the people you meet and the contacts you make.

Action Steps - The act of moving toward a desired state by making things real in stages; taking incremental actions toward goals and objectives.

Active Presentation - Consists of your name, business, profession, what you need to accomplish, and a brief description of what you do. An effective opening presentation is key to a successful first impression.

Act Like a Host - The act of receiving and entertaining guests in any setting.

Advice - Recommendation with regard to a course of action.

Affiliation - To connect or associate self with an individual or with a group.

Aim - To direct one's efforts. To direct to or towards a specific goal.

American Business Forum - A relationship building business conference that incorporates a relationship building mindset incorporating many of the principles of NetBeing.

Attuning - The preparation of being in harmony with your environment and with individuals within your environment.

B

Balanced Life - Considering all that is important to your life, i.e. family, physical health, spiritual life, career, relationships; making decisions that consider the whole of your life; not depriving one part of your life for the benefit of another part of your life.

Black Board Conferencing - Web based conferencing used widely in education and many other industries including research, science, and business; Telecommunications that supports discussions and text-based chats. Public postings to a blackboard around a specific theme. Brainstorming, debate, problem solving, information sharing, and learning initiatives are specific focuses a blackboard might encompass.

Building Context - Weaving related parts together to form and create a shared perspective; a process of gathering interrelated information and viewpoints to discover a common framework.

Building Tomorrow's Relationships Today - One's ability to assess past and present relationships and move these relationships forward purposefully.

Business like Person - One who is effective, efficient, practical and realistic in their attitudes and philosophies toward business interactions.

C

Casual Contacts - Acquaintances, customers, suppliers, and others that you meet for the first time. Generally people have more casual contacts in their inventory than strong contacts.

Cell Metaphor - Illustrates how human cells work together in an organized manner for the benefit of the total being contrasted to character traits which when working together in an organized manner optimize the benefits of the relationship.

Circle of Influence - Those things that a person can directly impact

Clarity - The quality or state of being clear.

Communication Channel - A path that one takes in transmitting one's intent and or to exchange information; channels include email, phone, video conferencing, mail, person-to-person.

Commitment - The act of committing, or the state of being committed; the act of pledging, obligating, or engaging oneself, as to taker on responsibility.

Connecting the Dots - Bringing together events and or information that helps to facilitate connection. It's not just making the connection, it's knowing what to do with the connection-connecting the dots along the way.

Connection - A meeting of another person at a feeling level forming a relationship connection that you sense relates to your intentions and purpose for your life.

Contact - An individual whom you consider to be a resource or are a resource for them.

Contactful - The art of making "good" contact with another person; a person's ability to facilitate a meeting with another that deepens the feeling connection inspiring you to go away from the meeting saying "I want to know this person."

Contact Fears - The fear that individuals may feel when meeting someone for the first time or going into a new setting.

Contact Spheres - Businesses or professions that naturally provide a flow of information or opportunity for one another. Contact spheres often occur in a clearly defined or related set of occupations.

Context - Context considers the environment, the situation, the relationship, and the language that supports the desired connection. Attention to context helps improve efficiency and effectiveness, directing and synthesizing communication to what is most important.

Context Awareness - The ability to "stay in context" with another or others, and not bring unrelated information or out-of-context conversation into the setting.

Cultivating - To foster the growth of something that is perceived to be in alignment with one's intention and or purpose.

D

Declaration of Interdependence - One's embracing that our independence is a direct result of our interdependence and cooperation with others.

Desire - A strong wish, longing or craving.

Determination - The act of moving through obstacles and challenges toward meeting goals and objectives.

Discernment - The quality of being able to sort through many variables to grasp and comprehend what is not readily obvious or visible.

Dream Fulfillment - Achievement of outcomes that one is passionate about.

Driving force - Something that motivates, excites, and inspires us.

E

Eight Magic Words of Networking - "I know someone that can get that done".

Empowerment - A sense of personal power in making decisions or having an impact on situations, organizations, and or individual influences.

Expert Systems - A computerized web source to go to obtain an area of excellence as it relates to one's knowledge of producing reliable and predicable results on a continuing basis. One's ability to reason , detect, diagnose, and respond to unusual situations, or to optimize processes in such industries such as manufacturing, telecommunications, transportation, aerospace and government. Expert systems are meant to solve real problems which normally would require a specialized human expert

External Life - The life one lives which consists of one's professional work, one's family, one's community that reflects one's internal state of being and internal self knowledge; identity that is reflected by outward personality.

F

Fishbone Diagram - Created by Kaoru Ishikawa to illustrate cause and effect and all the important factors key to successful performance for a given activity or project.

Five R's - A multitude of factors in our environment that support or distract from our relationship building activities. The 5 R's are foundational to the philosophy of NetBeing. They are rewardingness, reciprocity, rules, resourceful and relationshift.

Flow - To move in a natural rhythm with another individual, or the environment.

47-Second Networker - States that the optimum time of presenting yourself is 47 seconds to capture and maintain the listener's attention, before the listener shifts their attention to self or another person.

G

Gaudium - The word Joy comes from this Latin word meaning pleasure, gladness and happiness.

Gestalt - A German word meaning good form or plump wholeness, it is used in the world of personal growth and psychology to mean the ongoing process of completing "unfinished work" in order to move to wholeness within one's self. Unfinished business drains the energy we need for excitement, creativity, and making good contact in all realms of life. As we move in relationship with others, we continuously make good or unsatisfactory contact. Integrating gestalt into The Power Is In The Connection reinforces the act of awareness in the moment and encourages inquiry-what is needed now to make good contact with the person in front of me? What do I do now based on the unsatisfactory contact that has taken place? What are the range of tools and possibilities that can support wholeness and good contact between me and my partner? Gestalt is a relational approach of making good contact in the here and now!

Gestalt Psychotherapy - Gestalt therapy is an experiential process founded by Frederick (Fritz) and Laura Perls in the 1940s. The approach is to unblock the barriers to being fully alive and in the moment; the barriers of which were (and are) self constructed as a product of our family conditioning, society, education, and our environment. It is a process of growth in which individuals' awareness of moment to moment choice is distinguished from habitual living.

Giver's Gain Philosophy - A philosophy that states the way to get ahead is to help others get ahead. The philosophy supports the **Law of Reciprocity -** what goes around comes around.

Goals - The objectives you set for yourself aligned to your intentions and purpose.

Global Partner - A partnership that knows no geographical boundaries and holds to the tenants of the NetBeing philosophy.

Global Village - The entire world and its inhabitants.

Goldmine - Excellent computer software program for tracking the people you meet and the contacts you make.

H

Habit - An established pattern or way of thinking and doing things.

Hurried Society - A population of people who are highly attentive to time demands and constraints; individuals within society who are wrestling with many roles and responsibilities; a society of people having competing demands on their time with no clear purpose or intentions to help them guide their life

I

Imagination - The ability to visualize something in our mind beyond the present reality.

Influence - The ability to produce an affect based on one's personal characteristics such as displayed wisdom, inspirational, respecting and respectful, truthfulness, likeability, and charismatic power.

Integrity - Adherence to a code of values or ethics, established by culture, society, or business practices; may include sincerity, honesty and candor.

Intention - A determination to act in a certain way, such as to act with a specific purpose in mind.

Intentional Point - The point in which a decision is made based on choice and the intentions one holds.

Interdependent - Mutually dependent; the evolution of two or more interdependent species, each adapting to changes in the other. It occurs, for example, between predators and prey and between insects and the flowers that they pollinate.

Internal Life - The thoughts, the experiences, the fears, the conditioning, the dreams of the life within; the internal life is what is invisible to others unless shared verbally or non verbally; all of us live two lives: the inner life and the outer life.

Interrelated - Two or more distinctions that are interwoven based on a mutual relationship.

Intelligence of Attention - The ability to focus one's attention and stay focused toward the outcome you want for a dream, a project, or for a role you play such as successful parenting.

Intrapersonal - Existing or occurring within the individual's self or mind.

Interpersonal - Of or relating to the interactions between individuals; individual communication skills, both verbal and non verbal that bridge the gap between two or more people.
Invisible Support System - A belief in a higher force that we cannot see.

J

Joy - The emotion evoked by well-being, love, success, or good fortune.
Joyful Experience - A conscious positive perception of that leads to a good feeling for self and for the other; the act of providing or facilitating a state of joy for self and for another.
Just-In-Time-Knowledge - Facts, information or knowledge that is identified and usable at the very moment you need it.

K

Kaleidoscope - An instrument containing loose bits of colored material (as glass or plastic) between two flat plates and two plane mirrors so placed that changes of position of the bits of material are reflected in an endless variety of patterns.

L

Law of Attraction - You attract people, events and circumstances into your life that reflect your dominant thoughts and intentions; your being.
Law of Commitment - The level of commitment is the critical element that determines the long-term health and happiness of a relationship.
Law of Persistence - Your ability to persist in the face of inevitable set-backs and disappointments is the measure of your belief in yourself and your ability to succeed.
Law of Reciprocity - You are strongly motivated to "give back" for what you have received.
Legendary Status - To go above and beyond the expectations of others; so much so, that people can't help but talk about you.
Liberating Realizations - Freeing self up to letting go and moving on while recreating a relationship vision with the same person; letting go of preconceived ideas or expectations of what another person should do or be based on your own desires or wishes.
Life Purpose - Your mission for your life; that which is most important to you.

M

Memory Hook - An image, slogan, or tangible gift useful for helping others remember your name, product or business.

Mindful - A process of attentiveness and focus.

Mindfulness - A state of being mindful; mindfulness considers the dynamic complexity of individuals and the ongoing moment to moment relational process as one moves forward into a genuine encounter with another toward "good" contact.

Mission - Purpose for your life, your reason for being.

Multiple Visions - The many ways you see your life's intentions: your vision as parent, your vision for your career or multiple career paths, your vision for your spiritual life and overall health, and your vision for relationships.

Mutual Success - Success for the other as well as success for yourself.

N

NetBeing - A new word coined to capture the essence of a relationship mindset and a way of life; a way of being in relationship from an inside out view of the world; a philosophy based on intention and attention.

NetBeing Process - Goes beyond networking whereby individual purposes overlap and a joint focus fosters mutual success. NetBeing transforms networking contacts to a relationship focus through person-to-person connection.

Net Profits - Equity that begins to build in a network as you begin to give to others.

Network - An interconnected or interrelated group of people linked to one another through varied interests.

Network Conductor - Special software developed to power a seating rotation that systematically brings people together.

Networking - A process that helps us make contact with others, and gain access to information and resources.

Networking Attitude - The way you think about the development of relationships within the various networks that support you and others.

Networking Process - Provides a situational focus to gain personal success and for individuals to connect with others to achieve mutual goals.

Networking Strategy - The science and art of utilizing networking principles through a careful plan or method.

New Intelligence - Enhanced thinking about what you already know.

Next Level - The level up from where you are currently as you think about relationship.

Nonverbal Communication - Process of communication based on voice intonation, word choice, volume, speed, inflection, and body language.

O

Objective - Something toward which effort is directed: an aim, goal, or end state.

One-Minute Phone Net Strategy - Effective telephone communication technique for Networking professionals. A one-minute telephone strategy based on the needs of two people.

Openness - Receptive to ideas and people's feelings.

P

Passion - Intense, driving, overmastering feeling that moves through and with you. Strong feelings, emotions, or enthusiasm about something that you do and believe in.

Personal History - Interaction that has taken place between two people over a period of time. This interaction is part of the process that helps in the building of a solid relationship.

Personal Mastery - The ability to manage and lead oneself.

Positivity - The quality or state of being positive, in ways we connect rather then focusing on individual differences that disconnect us.

Process - A natural phenomenon marked by gradual changes that moves one forward in life, in relationship, or toward a particular result. We cannot help but be "in process."

Pro-active Approach - Increasing the probability through the development of a relationship mindset that someone will want to interact with you.

Pro-ject - A process by which we imagine forward a possible outcome; a process of forward looking.

Project - An undertaking, tangible plan, or design that casts us forward; a process of forward action toward a small or large activity.

Purposeful Listening - Listening with your five senses, and with your heart, mind and soul.

Purposefully - An object or result aimed at intention, resolution, and determination. Are you living your life purposefully?

R

Reciprocity - The giving and receiving that creates a sense of balance and a sense of mutuality.

Relationshift - The process of transforming a relationship as the focus of the relationship changes. The re-identifying of the existing relationship as it flows into something else. The act of identifying and transforming your thoughts and your view of an existing relationship.

Relationship - A flow of feelings between two people.

Relationship Attitude - An attitude of mindfulness toward the development of relationship.

Relationship Builder - A process of focusing on strategies, techniques, and processes to develop relationship.

Relationship Focus - Focuses on relationship as the heart of all success in life.

Relationship Mindset - Thinking process that guides the development of relationship and helps you diagnose the appropriate relationship strategy.

Relationship Rules - To reinforce that each of us brings rules to the relationship based on many personal factors. Rules are constantly changing as the relationship changes; some relationship rules may be formal or contractual.

Relationship Society - People intentionally getting together to build relationships.

Relationship Strategy - The notion of a strategic focus relating to the delivery of value to another person. A plan of action with the relationship in mind.

Relationship Strategies Institute - An organization responsible for delivering programming behind this book. A skills training institute that supports the relationship strategies and the NetBeing philosophy.

Relevance - The ability to retrieve material that satisfies the end user.

Resolution of Mission - A formal statement expressing your will and your intent.

Resource - Any source of aid or support. Being resourceful is an important characteristic for strengthening relationships.

Resourceful - Able to meet situations. Capable of devising ways and means to help self and to help others.

Resourcefulness - The ability to effectively and efficiently respond to problems, determine resources that are important.

Responsiveness - Quick to respond or react appropriately.

Rewarding - A sense of reward or worthwhile return.

Rewardingness - An ongoing exchange and satisfaction based on mutual benefits for all.
Rules - Internal and external guides for conduct that individually influence our engagement with others.

S

Self Knowledge - Understanding of how you work internally as well as externally; understanding your process, pattern recognition, thinking, what motivates, and what triggers you.
Shared Extraordinary - The formula (commitment + understanding + relationship passion) for relationship success is a foundation for exceeding one's expectations in interactions.
Shared Focus - A leader's ability to focus and project intention and vision to help team members in their ability to be creative and develop an organizational presence. Individuals are aligned with each other and the process of which helps them more effortlessly accomplish objectives.
Shared History - The sharing of personal and business information over a period of time.
Shorten Learning Curves - The ability to bring prior and joint learning to the situation or project and diminish long processes of rediscovery or reinvention.
Six Degrees of Separation - Hypothesis that everyone in the world can be connected by six degrees of separation. Four words that describe the phenomenon of a shrinking world where any random two people can discover a link through a chain of six acquaintances.
Small World Theory - This theory states that everything we come in contact with can be reduced to a small world if we recall previous experiences and interactions then understand what to do with the information.
Spiral of Continuous Learning - A continuous forward learning process that takes one back to a focal point from start to finish, aligning the skill set and considering the impact of choices on the many intentions for one's life to one focal point, that is to live one's life purposefully.
Speed of Business - One's ability to focus attention, energy, and resources to respond quickly to the objectives at hand; to eliminate distractions that detract from joint endeavors.
Still Place Within - A sense of peace overcomes the sense of anxiety and uncertainty. This is achieved when one takes a step back to contemplate and reflect on the situation and go to one's quiet inner source.

Strong Contacts - Personal, family members, partners and close business or networking associates whereby individuals have a genuine loyalty to each other. People generally have fewer strong contacts than casual contacts.
Strategic Focus - Concentration toward the completion of a strategic plan.
Synchronicity - Meaningful coincidences that occur when aligned intentions result in serendipitous meetings and occurrences.
Synergy - The result of two or more people producing together more than the sum of what they could produce separately.
System - A group of interacting, interrelated, or interdependent elements forming a complex whole.
A condition of harmonious, orderly interaction. An organized and coordinated method; a procedure

T

Taking the moment and dancing with it - Is an opportunity for an individual to stop and think about what is happening in the moment, and making the most of it.
Targeted Visibility - Increase opportunities to meet people with specific interests or fields.
Technologically Savvy - An understanding of the technology available and its importance toward moving your relationship, your project, and your organization forward.
Tele-Magic - An excellent computer software program for tracking the people you meet and the contacts you make.
Time Alignment - Allocating and aligning time to that which is most important to you.
Training and Development Resources, Inc. - An organization founded by Jane George-Surges in 1996 delivering programming behind this book. A relationship focused skills training institute focusing on culture, leadership, and partnership.
Triple Win Theory - A theory that states three people can win in any interaction or encounter. Typically presents itself when referrals are given or someone is identified as a resource.

U

Unparalleled Visibility - Optimized visibility that supports all aspects of your life.

V

Velocity - Quickness of motion in a given direction.

Video Conferencing - Teleconferencing for the purpose of meetings, interaction and information sharing; used widely in education for giving and receiving courses.

Virtual Offices - Office is identified by you; portable and flexible, anywhere, anytime.

Vision - A mental image created by the imagination.

W

Winning Relationship - A relationship of mutual support: one where the objective is to support the efforts of each other.

INDEX

A

B

C

J

K

L

M

N

O

P

R

How to reach Ron Sukenick

Ron Sukenick is the President and Creator of The Relationship Strategies Institute, a global enterprise committed to providing information and skills for individuals wishing to take their personal and professional relationships to the Next*Level.*

The Relationship Strategies Institute is a training and business development company that provides innovative, effective and relevant programs and systems for corporations, organizations and associations.

Ron is a widely recognized speaker and trainer whose presentations are known for their practical information, humor and results. Visit the two web-sites below for additional information:

www.RelationshipStrategiesInstitute.com
www.NetBeing.us

please contact me at
(317) 216-8210
rs@relationshipstrategiesinstititute.com

How to reach Jane George-Surges, SPHR

A dynamic process of relationship as primary to individual and organizational success has been at the heart of Training and Development Resources, Inc. since its inception in 1996. Gestalt psychology, systems thinking, organizational development, and skills as a senior professional in human resources thread throughout the work of the practice.

Shifting relationships as they change personally or professionally is one of the biggest challenges most of us face! How to navigate between who we are as individuals and our connectedness to others is a delicate balance.

Let me know how I or my associates can help you or your organization better navigate and create leadership, high performance team development, collaborations, conflict resolution, and creating an organizational culture of relationship. Customized training and speaking engagements are available.

Regardless, now that we have a relationship, let's stay in touch! I invite you to email me and share your stories, your challenges, and your relationship insights.

Please contact me directly at jgsurges@aol.com or visit the two web-sites below for additional information:

www.trainingdevelopmentresources.com
www.netbeing.us
(317) 920-0188

I look forward to hearing from you!